THE ART OF

HAPPY

MOVING

THE ART OF

HAPPY

MOVING

How to Declutter, Pack, and Start Over While
Maintaining Your Sanity and Finding Happiness

ALI WENZKE

wm

WILLIAM MORROW
An Imprint of HarperCollins*Publishers*

HarperCollins books may be purchased for educational, business, or sales promotional use. For information, please email the Special Markets Department at SPsales@harpercollins.com.

FIRST EDITION

Designed by Fritz Metsch
Illustrations by Lise Sukhu

Library of Congress Cataloging-in-Publication Data has been applied for.

ISBN 978-0-06-286973-9

19 20 21 22 23   LSC   10 9 8 7 6 5 4 3 2 1

To Victoria, Joseph, and Charlotte,
you are my happiness.

To Daniel,
you are my everything.

CONTENTS

INTRODUCTION

Moving at any time—and especially with kids—is one of Dante's official circles of hell. It's true. It gets lost in translation, but if you look at the original *Inferno* it reads:

Following the ninth circle of hell,
therein lies the most terrible place of all.
'Tis where one must pack up her entire life
while keeping the house so clean for showings
that no one would ever imagine
rambunctious children with hordes of toys
sprawled everywhere moments before.

It's more lyrical in Italian.

I've been there. Many times, in fact. My husband, Dan, and I moved ten times in eleven years and added three kids into the mix along the way. Sure, moving is a challenge, but it's also doable. This book will show you not only how to survive a move, but how to make the most of it.

Of course, Happy Moving doesn't mean you'll skip and whistle as you pack your boxes. Happy Moving means remembering to laugh because, sometimes, that's all you can do. It means maximizing the highs and minimizing the lows. Most important, Happy Moving means finding ways to be better off *after* the move than you were before.

I'm not going to lie. Moving *does* include some rough patches. The time Dan and I moved from Ohio to California springs to mind. We had decided to tow our Honda Passport behind a U-Haul truck, cinching a canvas cover over the top (we didn't want to scrape 2,500 miles of bugs off the windshield when we arrived in Palo Alto). It was a genius innovation. We exchanged high fives and knowing looks and put that truck into gear. Killing it.

About a mile and a half onto the highway, Dan noticed that the U-Haul seemed unstable. Was a crosswind hitting the truck's side? Was there a storm coming in?

Not a cloud in the sky.

Passing cars honked at us, but as far as we were concerned we were still killing it. I mean, come on, people—moving trucks are bound to be slow. *Just go around!* Finally, a guy in a Toyota Camry pulled alongside and rolled down his window. Unable to yell over the roar of the open road, he pointed to our trailer and shook his head, eyes wide, then zoomed away.

Dan checked the side mirror. The Honda on its trailer swerved in and out of view.

Swerved in and out of view?! Within seconds, the tail jerked the front of the truck, whipping us across the highway like a gigantic, hungry cobra. I gripped the door handle as we careened to the shoulder, and somehow we managed *not* to flip over our U-Haul in the middle of I-80.

We learned something that day: a canvas car cover makes an impressive parachute.

Throughout this book, I'll reveal even more poor choices we made while moving. Maybe you, and the thirty-five million other people who move in the United States every year, can save yourselves from these types of—*ahem*—genius innovations.

The average American moves 11.7 times in a lifetime, so you've probably racked up a crazy story or two of your own. Hopefully you've had your share of Happy Moving moments, too, like the time we bought a town house over coffee and muffins (without any real estate agents involved). Still, my favorite stories are the absurd ones, absurd in the way only moving can be. Maybe you battled a biblical plague of grasshoppers while passing through Iowa like we did. No? Just us?

Moving means you get to create unforgettable memories, and it also means you get the chance to start over so you can live an even happier life. According to happiness researchers and psychologists, 50 percent of our happiness is genetic.* So, worst case scenario, you were born 50 percent grumpy. I can work with that. Another 10 percent of our happiness comes from our life circumstances, and since you're reading this book, your life circumstances might be a bit stressful at the moment. I can help you out. Moving logistics, packing and decluttering, making sure your favorite pet doesn't get lost . . . we'll cover it all, a little at a time.

The final 40 percent of the happiness pie is how you look at the world—your attitude and your personal outlook, and how they influence your actions. This is where we'll work on

---

* S. Lyubomirsky, K. M. Sheldon, and D. Schkade, "Pursuing Happiness: The Architecture of Sustainable Change," *Review of General Psychology,* 9(2005): pp. 111–131.

the happily-ever-after part, something that'll stick around long after your move. I'll guide you through what researchers say you need to be happier and what things don't matter that much. We'll focus on ways to be happier at home and outside the home. We'll talk about how to make friends and get connected to your community, because social relations are important. It's hard to be happy without at least one good one. I'll give you tips and strategies for how to build your community when you start from scratch.

It's time to pull out my 5-Step Road Map to Happy Moving. Here we go.

STEP 1: CHANGE YOUR MINDSET

People say moving is one of life's most stressful events, but it doesn't have to be. Let's rebrand it and focus on the fresh start. Moving—even if it's down the block—is the perfect time to start over and make changes in your life. A positive attitude and an altered outlook on moving itself will help.

STEP 2: SET GOALS

When you start over, you can be anyone you want to be, and the good news is that the laws of habit formation are on your side. As we'll discuss in chapter 13, more than one-third of people who made lasting habit changes attributed their success to moving somewhere new. That's a mind-blowing head start, and you don't need to do one extra thing. Simply proceed with your move. This is a chance to restart your life, and those don't come around every day. We'll cover goal-setting and moving resolutions later in the book because you've got some moving to do and you may be short on time.

STEP 3: SIMPLIFY THE LOGISTICS

Packing, movers, storage, pets, the kids, procrastinating over a box of old photos for two hours, home showings . . . it's a lot to think about. That's where I come in. I'll share my simple checklists and creative ideas for how to pack, declutter, and organize. If you want inspirational and/or head-scratcher stories about what *not* to do, I have those, too. For the detail-oriented, Type A, worry-a-holic types, don't worry—you're in good company. I tucked in some epic to-do lists just for you in the appendix. And if you're not? That's okay. I'll cover the basics throughout the book.

STEP 4: PREPARE YOUR FAMILY FOR THE MOVE

If you're like many parents I talk to, your top concern is . . . your kids. How do we talk to our kids about moving? Will my son fit in? How will my daughter cope in a different school? I can guide you through this. This topic is so near and dear to me that I host family workshops to help kids through the transition. It's remarkable how a child's confidence can grow in a one-hour workshop. You can teach your own kid these tips at home with the role-playing scenarios you'll read about in chapter 16. Also, despite what your kids may tell you, you are not ruining their lives. Just so you know.

STEP 5: FOCUS ON BUILDING A COMMUNITY

When I moved to Knoxville, it took me a long, *long* time to find that initial good, solid friend. After so many moves, this dry spell was a first for me and I felt, well, lonely. My loneliness was profound and unexpected. It changed me. It became the inspiration for my work on moving and the driving force behind this book. In chapters 14 to 16 I'll share my hard-won strategies for how to make a good first impression and turn acquaintances into friends so that you don't find yourself in the same lonely situation I once did.

There is an art to Happy Moving, and everybody's happy move looks different. Together, we'll figure out what *you* need to be happy.

1

IS MOVING THE RIGHT CALL FOR YOU?

Life Check

Raising children in New York City is just stupid. So why do we stay in New York City? . . . I belong in New York City. I need New York City's energy, diversity, and the convenience. Sometimes I leave for work ten minutes before I have to be onstage. I don't want to give that up.

—JIM GAFFIGAN, *Dad Is Fat*

You might be asking yourself, "Do I really have to do this?"

Or, put in a less angsty way, "Is this move right for me?"

Well, not all moves are created equal, and sometimes a great city may not be so great for you. Let's take Knoxville, Tennessee, for example. *U.S. News & World Report* has ranked Knoxville as one of the "125 Best Places to Live in the USA." In 2018, Knoxville landed at #64, beating out big city rivals like New York City, Chicago, and Miami. It also beat Tucson, Santa Barbara, and Tampa, to name a few. Knoxville is a solid, midsize city with nice people and good weather. All the stats are there. On paper, anyone would love living in Knoxville. Anyone would be happy there. But we didn't, and we weren't.

Looking back, it's clear what my husband and I did wrong.

Dan and I evaluated the *city* before we moved, but we didn't evaluate *ourselves*. Take a look at the Pros and Cons list we made before heading to Knoxville, which I've reproduced here.

MOVING TO KNOXVILLE

PROS	CONS
Great job offer	Leaving our friends
Lower cost of living	Leaving our walkable neighborhood
No state income tax	We'll miss Broadway in Chicago
Mild climate	We'll miss the Mexican and Indian restaurants
Good place to raise kids	We'll miss the Chicago Air and Water Show
Can afford nice home	We'll miss the beach and outdoor festivals
Near Smoky Mountains	
No more dealing with city problems	

Based on this list, the choice seemed like a no-brainer. Dan and I didn't second-guess our decision to leave Chicago. In fact, we couldn't wait to make Knoxville our forever home, where we would raise our kids and grow old together.

Then we moved. The joy I got from the mountains and lakes in Knoxville didn't balance out the isolation I felt at our house in the suburbs. In Chicago, I could walk out my front door and run into another mom pushing a stroller within minutes. In Knoxville, we found ourselves oddly out of step: our kids were still in diapers while all the neighbors had teenagers on high school sports teams. I thought I had wanted the big house in the suburbs, but I didn't realize how lonely suburban living could be. A lot of deep thinking followed this realization, and despite our best efforts to make the most of our situation, we ultimately decided that Knoxville wasn't right for us. The cost of living was lower than in Chicago, but having more money in our pockets didn't amount to greater happiness for me or my family.

Traveling through Dante's circles of hell just to land in a place that doesn't work out seems, well . . . suboptimal. If we had done a better job evaluating our likes and dislikes, we might have avoided the hassle of moving to a place that wasn't a good fit. Figuring out if you're going to like a city before you move there requires foresight and soul-searching. Learn from our mistakes: evaluate yourself first.

Here's a quick exercise to help you identify what's most important to you. Rank only the five most important items from those listed. You can ignore the rest. Go ahead, I'll wait.

Most Important Things in My Life
(Use a scale of 1 to 5 and rank only your top five.)

___ A successful career

___ Financial wealth

___ Close personal relationships

___ A nice home

___ Religion or spirituality

___ Hobbies or leisure activities

___ Intellectual growth

___ Safety

___ Autonomy

___ Helping others

___ Being healthy

Now, pick the main reason you are moving and write it here: _____ .

I know we move for a combination of reasons, but you only get to pick one. So, dig deep and pick the most important reason.

If the main reason you're moving isn't in your top five, then this decision is easy. If it's up to you, don't move. It's not worth it. Simple. Just close this book and head to the beach. (Sorry, no refunds.)

For example, if you're moving for a higher-paying job, but money and wealth aren't high on your list, then the odds your move will make you happier are low. What about the opposite situation? Your top priority is career advancement, but you plan to put your career on hold to be closer to extended family. Be honest about what your values are before you make yourself (and maybe the whole family?) miserable.

That said, sometimes the decision isn't just about you. It's also about the needs of others, people whose values and dreams don't perfectly line up with yours. So, let's delve deeper with the following fun quiz. If someone else is moving with you, have him or her join in. You might learn something about each other in the process.

SELF-EVALUATION QUIZ

1. **If you could be one of these TV show/movie characters, who would you want to be?**

   a. Carrie Bradshaw in *Sex and the City*
   b. Madeline Martha Mackenzie in *Big Little Lies*
   c. Cheryl Strayed in *Wild*
   d. George Bailey in *It's a Wonderful Life*

2. **What does your ideal Saturday look like?**

   a. Listening to a popular local band
   b. Doing a fix-it project that works on the first try
   c. Going for a hike through the woods
   d. Watching the big game at home with friends

3. **When someone visits from out of town, you want to:**

   a. Show her the newest exhibit at the museum
   b. Paint together at a local art studio
   c. Walk along the riverfront
   d. Test out your latest pasta Bolognese recipe at home

4. **You pour yourself a coffee on a Monday morning. You look out your kitchen window, thrilled to see:**

   a. A city skyline
   b. Your herb garden on the patio
   c. The mountains in the distance
   d. The open countryside

5. **You're excited because your friend just called with an invitation to:**

   a. See *Hamilton*
   b. Grab a drink at a neighborhood bar
   c. Go paddleboarding
   d. Play *Cards Against Humanity* with a close group of friends

6. **You can't imagine life without:**

   a. A stack of take-out menus from nearby ethnic food restaurants
   b. Your kid's weekend soccer games
   c. Easy access to a running path or a bike trail
   d. A quiet, solitary place to think

7. **Your ideal commute would be:**

   a. Walking through city streets and occasionally using public transportation
   b. Taking a train, so you can get downtime before and after work
   c. Bike riding on a clear day
   d. Driving to work over rolling hills with little traffic

8. **It's Sunday brunch. Where do you imagine yourself?**

   a. At the newest brunch place, sipping mimosas
   b. At a cozy pancake restaurant with a hot cup of coffee
   c. At the beach with a picnic basket
   d. At your house with a simple breakfast and a good book

9. **You can't stand this (the most):**

   a. Having nowhere to go
   b. Small parking spaces
   c. Concrete
   d. Beeping trash trucks

10. **Your dream home is:**

   a. A luxury penthouse with a roof garden
   b. A house with a private office, home theater room, and three-car garage
   c. A cabin on a lake
   d. A house on a large plot of land where the nearest neighbor is acres away

Now tally up how many As, Bs, Cs, and Ds you picked.

If you scored highest on As, you love the energy of a big city. You're drawn to the bustle of living in a metropolis where people are active and going places. It makes you feel happy to be in the middle of the action. Anything less feels boring

If you scored highest on Bs, you like the occasional evening out, but you also enjoy the comforts of a more spacious home. You appreciate the ease of driving to nearby shopping or restaurants. It's important to have access to fun activities or cultural events, even if you don't always take advantage of them. Just knowing that they're an option is often enough.

If you scored highest on Cs, your ideal place gives you easy access to nature. You feel happiest outdoors. Living a healthy lifestyle and being around others who share a love of nature are important to you. There's nothing better than the smell of fresh air.

If you scored highest on Ds, you love peace and quiet. You'd choose a good book at home or a day watching TV over a five-star restaurant any day. You don't need the outside world to entertain you. Your family, friends, and home are all you need.

The results are in . . .

So, how'd you do? If you scored overwhelmingly high in one category, you may already know that you're either a city, suburbs, country, or nature kind of a person. If you're moving somewhere that's completely different from your personal style, it may be a more difficult transition for you (unless you're feeling adventurous). I'm not saying a city girl can never be happy in the country or a country guy can't be happy in the city, but it may be tough to acclimate if this is a fundamental part of who you are. Consider whether you're up for the challenge of trying something new, moving somewhere you'd feel out of place at first.

Chances are you got a smattering of As, Bs, Cs, and Ds. If so, consider yourself "flexible." Being adaptable is a good thing, especially when moving is concerned. Focus on the positives, and you can move just about anywhere and be happy.

To get an even clearer picture about how to find happiness after you move, consider your favorite aspects of your current location. What seems impossible to live without? Maybe you love to count stars from your backyard or you relish your morning walks to the neighborhood coffee shop.

A location-specific gratitude journal can help clarify what aspects of your current location are important to you. Spend a few days recording the things you are thankful for in your current home. Here's a sample page from mine.

TODAY

Today I feel grateful about living in the Chicago suburbs because:

I walked my kids to school this morning.

Neighbors smiled and said hi.

My kids are having fun at their after-school activities.

I can park my car in my own garage.

The kids and I can watch squirrels and bunnies playing in our yard.

I love the wholesomeness of today's school fair.

LOOKING FORWARD

Looking forward at the next few weeks, I'm excited about:

Running in a neighborhood 5K.

Watching my kids' soccer games and recitals.

Going for a family bike ride.

Spending a day at the beach and neighborhood pool.

Going to a Chicago museum.

Volunteering at Bernie's Book Bank.

Going to a U2 concert.

**Looking back at the last few months, I really
enjoyed:**

Inviting friends over for coffee.

Going to the Chicago Botanic Garden.

Hearing an author speak at the Book Stall.

Running to the beach.

Watching my kids play in their tree house.

Seeing Jerry Seinfeld perform at the Rosemont Theatre.

Spending a night out with friends at Zanies Comedy Club.

I love the walkability of our suburban Chicago neighborhood
and the proximity to Lake Michigan. I appreciate the comforts
of suburban living while enjoying the perks of the nearby city.
Knoxville offers the wholesome family life that I love in the
Chicago burbs, but it couldn't compete with the Chicago night-
life or sandy beaches, things I feel so grateful for today.

All right, your turn. Write down everything about your current spot that makes you happy and why you feel grateful to
live where you are right now.

GRATITUDE JOURNAL

TODY

Today I feel grateful about living in _____ because:

LOOKING FORWARD

Looking forward at the next few weeks, I'm excited about:

LOOKING BACK

. . . .

Looking back at the last few months, I really enjoyed:

_____

_____

_____

_____

_____

You've done some intense thinking in this chapter. You've taken a look at what your top priorities are, you've developed a good sense of what you like about your hometown, and now you're ready to add it up. Is moving a good idea? Find out by following your path on the Should I Move flowchart on the next page (and remember that positive mindset!).

Ready to move now? Great! But before you pack up the truck, you may want to visit your destination city first. In the next chapter, you'll find a sample weekend itinerary to help get your travel plans started.

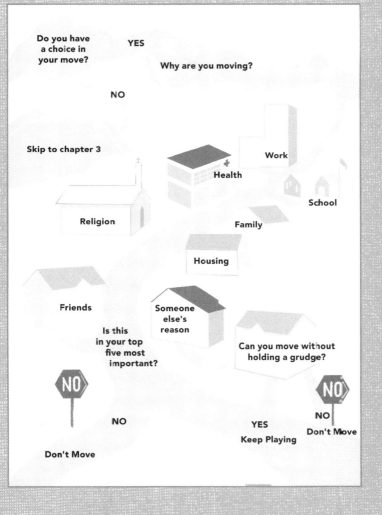

Do you have a choice in your move?

YES

Why are you moving?

NO

Skip to chapter 3

Work

Health

School

Religion

Family

Housing

Friends

Someone else's reason

Can you move without holding a grudge?

Is this in your top five most important?

NO

NO

Don't Move

YES
Keep Playing

NO
Don't Move

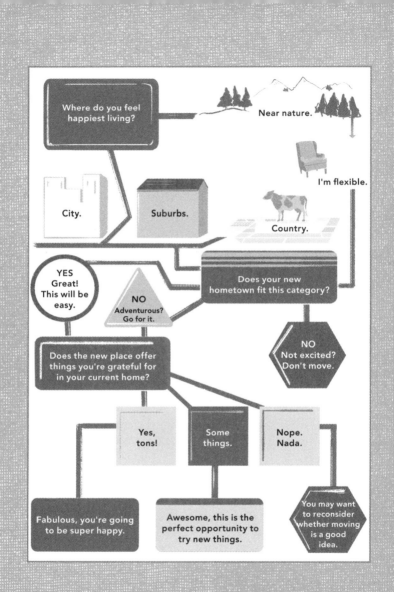

14

2

HOW TO EVALUATE A CITY BEFORE MOVING THERE

*Basically the only incentive a person needs to accept a
job is to be shown another job where the work is the same
but the pay is less. Then their job automatically becomes
what is referred to as "not a bad job." That's really all we
want—a "not a bad job"—and we're happy.*

—JERRY SEINFELD, *Sein Language*

Dan and I had our first date night in Knoxville almost six
months after we moved there. It was Dan's birthday and he
chose a charming French bistro not too far from our house.
With our three little munchkins safe at home with our first
local babysitter, we could enjoy each other's company—
uninterrupted—in a restaurant with white tablecloths and
candles. Life was good.

After warm Brie and a glass of wine, the conversation
shifted from mundane, everyday topics to what each of us
wanted out of life. The more we spoke, the more questions and
concerns began to spill out. Had we made the right decision
by moving to Knoxville? Was this where we wanted to raise
the kids? How *was* the job going, really? We had remained
positive in the six months since we'd arrived, giving the city a

fair chance. After all, it takes time to acclimate to a new place. Still, we couldn't ignore where this discussion was heading: Knoxville wouldn't be the long-term place for us.

It was time to start the city search again. We had become quite the pros by this point. While I didn't have any quizzes to guide me through the city evaluation, given how unhappy I felt in Knoxville, it was easy to pinpoint the missing things that *did* make me happy. I was able to learn from my own mistakes, and this time I knew exactly what I needed in a city.

So, how *do* you evaluate a city ahead of time? How can you avoid relocating to a place that isn't right for you? The first thing you can do is evaluate your life priorities and fill out a location-specific gratitude journal like we did in the previous chapter. The next step is to create a killer game plan and actually go visit the city on a weekend tour.

Take a look at the following sample itinerary for a long weekend visit. Okay, sure, it's an extra-long weekend, but there's a lot you'll want to see (and not everything is open on the weekend). Be sure to bring your camera and a notebook.

Sometimes we get only one chance to visit a city before we need to decide whether to uproot our lives to move there. If this is your predicament, here are a few general tips to help you maximize your visit:

- Research as much as you can before you go. The more research you do ahead of time, the more productive your trip will be.
- Take pictures of *everything*. Before you enter an apartment, take an outdoor shot, preferably with the

SAMPLE ITINERARY FOR
VISITING YOUR NEW CITY

THURSDAY P.M.	Arrive at new city
	Stay in an Airbnb or VRBO, if possible
	Eat dinner at locals' favorite restaurant
FRIDAY A.M.	Commute to work during rush hour
	Meet coworkers
FRIDAY P.M.	Eat casual lunch
	Plan 1–3 school/daycare visits
	Visit 1–2 housing options
	Go out for your ideal Friday night (see Gratitude Journal in chapter 1)
SATURDAY A.M.	Check out the local coffee shop
	Get groceries
	If you have kids, check out kids' sport facilities or attend a game
SATURDAY P.M.	Visit 2–5 housing options
	Have a picnic lunch at a local attraction

	Go out for your ideal Saturday night (see Gratitude Journal in chapter 1)
SUNDAY A.M.	Enjoy your ideal Sunday morning breakfast (see Gratitude Journal in chapter 1)
	Attend religious services, if applicable
	Walk through neighborhoods you're considering
	Go to a home improvement store or garden center
	Visit medical facilities, if this is a concern
SUNDAY P.M.	Check out open houses, even if you don't plan on buying a home
	Stop by Target or Walmart to buy a souvenir
	Go see a movie
MONDAY A.M.	If you have kids, go through a school drop-off line or visit a daycare
	Commute to work during rush hour
	Plan 1–3 school/daycare visits
MONDAY P.M.	Eat lunch at a restaurant near work

	Visit 2–5 housing options
	Mail a letter from the post office
	Check out the local library
	Make the commute from work back to home
TUESDAY A.M.	Tie up loose ends
	Revisit any schools, housing, or facilities as needed
	Eat lunch at a favorite local spot
TUESDAY P.M.	Return home

building name or address showing. If you have a housing listing sheet, take a picture of that, too. These photos will act as dividers to help you keep the details straight. The pictures will also help you plan your furniture arrangements from afar.

· Take videos so you can see how the pictures fit together.
· Take notes. Jot down any impressions you may have or practical details you notice while you explore.

In the next section I provide answers to some more specific concerns that may arise as you evaluate a city.

ACCOMMODATIONS DURING YOUR VISIT

Should I stay at an Airbnb/VRBO or a hotel?

I recommend an Airbnb or VRBO, if possible. When you stay at a hotel, you see the city as a tourist. If you stay in a neighborhood home, you get a better perspective of what it's like to be a local. If you can't rent a place for the weekend, get a hotel in or near the neighborhood you're most seriously considering.

What if I can't visit for more than two days?

If you're working within a tight time frame, then try to visit on a weekday *and* a weekend day. A tranquil Sunday afternoon is different than a busy Monday morning.

THE COMMUNITY

Should I grocery shop and go to Target when I'm on my visiting vacation?

Yes. Also, you're not on vacation. This is a work trip. Your job is to see if you'd like living in this place on a daily basis. You'll learn much more from the checkout line at Target than you will from a visit to the Space Needle.

How do I choose a church, synagogue, or mosque?

Ask your current religious community for recommendations. Friends, real estate agents , and the forums on City-Data.com can be good options to help you get started, too. Stop in for services at a few different places before you commit.

Should I go to the local library?

Absolutely. You can get free stuff and librarians are awesome. Tell the librarian you are considering relocating to the area and ask if she can tell you about the library services. You may find out about free museum passes for residents or upcoming library events or free streaming sites. Better yet, it's a chance to chat with a knowledgeable local.

How do I find fun activities to do in town?

Go back to your Gratitude Journal from chapter 1 as a reminder of what you love to do. Then, look at the city's online weekend calendar to seek out your favorite types of activities. Check out the latest movie, a concert, or a high school football game.

Visit TripAdvisor and Yelp to choose what attractions and restaurants you'd most like to visit on a typical Saturday. If you're moving to Orlando, you probably won't be going to Disney World every weekend, so see what else is popular with people who live there. Where would you go for a quick meal on a Thursday night? Try to live your future life. There'll be time for the touristy stuff later.

THE JOB

While evaluating your new city is important, you are probably evaluating your job opportunities as well. Research about your job will most likely begin before your trip, but you can gather useful information during your weekend visit to help you make an informed decision on whether to move for the job.

How can I learn about the company's culture before I visit?

College alumni groups and online resources like LinkedIn and Glassdoor can help. Check out the websites and social media accounts of your future employer to see if your personal views and career goals align with the company's brand. Speak with current employees whenever possible to find out what daily life is like. What do people like about working there? What needs improvement?

Any tips on evaluating my workplace?

If you already have a job offer, ask your human resources contact if you can get an office tour when you are in town to visit the city. Scope out the people and your work space. Do you like a quiet place with few interruptions or a more social and collaborative environment? Have lunch with your future colleagues, not just the hiring manager. How well do people seem to get along with one another? If you don't have a job lined up yet, reach out to professional contacts or ask someone in human resources at a company you're interested in if you can set up an informational meeting to learn more about the company and potential hiring opportunities.

How important is my commute?

VERY. If you want to sabotage your happiness, sign up for a long commute to work. A long commute affects your overall life satisfaction and well-being—not to mention your family's happiness. Please don't underestimate the importance of commuting. I recommend a dry run during rush hour to get an accurate representation of what traffic will be like before moving forward with any short-term or long-term real estate decisions.

SCHOOLS

How can I learn about schools in the area?

For test scores, class sizes, and student demographics, you can check out websites like SchoolDigger and GreatSchools.* To get more details, you can ask a Realtor or any friends or friends of friends who know the area. It's easy to connect with locals online through the forums on City-Data.com. This site connects local residents with people like you who are considering a move, and you'll find every U.S. state and many

* Links to these sites can be found on the Resources page of my website, at www.artofhappymoving.com/resources.

international locations represented. Read through the forum threads and if you don't find the information you need, post your own question to ask about your specific concerns. What kind of aftercare programs are there? Do kids walk to school or take a bus? How involved are the parents in the school?

Can I schedule tours with schools?

It depends on individual policies, but it doesn't hurt to contact the school office to ask about tours. If you have questions, write them down so you remember to ask them during the tour. It's much easier to talk to someone in person than over email or even on the phone. If you are able to take a school tour, ask if there's a current parent who'd be willing to chat during your visit or answer follow-up questions. Remember to take notes and pictures as details can blend together or be forgotten later.

INITIAL HOUSING IN YOUR NEW CITY

Sites like Realtor.com, Zillow, Redfin, and Apartments.com make it easy to start your housing search before your weekend visit. Add the homes you love to your "favorites" list, and then check them out in person when you visit. Be sure to consider the following details as you begin your search.

Should I buy or rent?

Rent. There, I said it. Unless you know a city well and are extremely confident about finding or liking a new job, you should rent. Renting gives you the opportunity to check out neighborhoods, settle into your work space, and get a feel for the local area. Your idea of the dream neighborhood might be different after a few months in town. Also, renting protects you from having to sell a house if your job doesn't work out for some reason.

If I rent, doesn't that mean I need to move twice?

Yes, it does. If you plan to buy a home eventually, it does mean moving twice. Not ideal, I know, but neither is getting stuck with a mortgage if the job falls through or if you realize that the best schools are two miles in the other direction. Consider it insurance. To be fair, it's more like moving one and a half times instead of twice. If you plan on a short-term rental, you can pack in phases. Find a place to store items you can live without for a while (furniture or your holiday decorations). Unpack only the items you really need. When we moved to our rental house in the Chicago suburbs, we unpacked just the essentials, and it felt freeing to live more simply.

Should I pick the nicer house or the nicer neighborhood?

A bigger home doesn't correlate to a higher level of happiness, but having a better community almost universally does. Focus on finding the right neighborhood first and *then* choose your house or apartment.

What should I look for in a neighborhood?

Look for highly rated schools, neighbors at a similar life stage, sidewalks, access to nature, and a decent commute time. Even if you don't have kids, you'll want to consider the schools if you plan to buy a home because the school district can impact a house's resale value. In terms of access to nature, look for mature trees near your home or an outdoor courtyard or a place where you can get fresh air and sunshine. You can also check out the Walk Score of any housing you are considering. The Walk Score is a cool piece of data that measures the walkability of any address, scoring it from 0 (poor walkability) to 100 (walker's paradise). Find out how easy it is to grab lunch, buy groceries, or enjoy local entertainment without getting into your car.

EXERCISE: CLOSE YOUR EYES AND IMAGINE YOUR NEW LIFE

Imagine waking up in a new house. You get ready for the day and if you have kids, they get ready, too. How does everyone get to where they're going? Who will you interact with along the way? Think of your neighbors, the daycare workers, and other commuters. You walk into your office and greet your co-workers. How does it feel? What are they like? You head home during rush hour. How long is the ride? Do you grab dinner on the way home or stop at the grocery store? After dinner you have a moment to relax. What do you want to do? What are your plans for the weekend?

Open your eyes and reflect. Some routines will feel familiar to you, but there will be changes after you move. Do you find these differences exciting or do you dread them? We each have distinct dreams. Whether it's the high energy of a big city or a quiet life in the country, be honest about what seems best for you. Think past the higher pay or the fancy house to what will actually bring you happiness.

The reality is that there is no Shangri-la. Otherwise, we'd all want to live there. Plus, the cost of living would be astronomical. Every move has its trade-offs. Our job is to get as close to great as possible.

Some of you may need to buy or sell your house before you move. If a real estate transaction is in your future, then carry on to the next chapter. If not, skip ahead to chapter 5, where you'll learn the first secret to Happy Moving: get rid of everything you own.

3

COMMON MISTAKES MADE BY FIRST-TIME HOME BUYERS

LUCY: *I know how you feel about all this Christmas business, getting depressed and all that. It happens to me every year. I never get what I really want. I always get a lot of stupid toys or a bicycle or clothes or something like that.*
CHARLIE BROWN: *What is it you want?*
LUCY: *Real estate.*

— CHARLES M. SCHULZ, *A Charlie Brown Christmas*

I've made three big home-buying mistakes in my life. The first mistake was falling in love with a house when I should've played it cool. My second big mistake was being that nitpicky buyer, the one that no one wants to deal with because she haggles over every detail. And finally, the worst offense of all: I bought a house in a city that I knew virtually nothing about. Oh, young Ali. You had so much to learn.

BIG HOME-BUYING MISTAKE #1

Early in our marriage, Dan and I lived in different cities while I pursued a law degree and he completed his medical degree, and later his residency. After years of buying plane tickets, we could finally abandon the Ohio-California/California-Illinois commute. Thrilled at the prospect of a more traditional living arrangement, we decided to search for the perfect home in Chicago.

And we found it. The *perfect* town house. One of a kind, unlikely to ever be on the market again, so hot people were probably bidding on it right then as we waited for the bank to approve our loan. The brick facade! The sunny living room! The neighborhood! We might never find anything so amazingly perfect ever again.

Yup, you guessed it: we were in love.

Here's the problem with falling in love . . . it makes us kind of dumb. We're willing to overlook flaws because, you know, it's *love*. It didn't matter that the bathroom countertops were below my waist level (I'm five two), meaning Dan would probably need to sit down to brush his teeth comfortably. Sure, the kitchen was outdated and the sellers had strategically placed potted plants and rugs to hide the floor damage. *Eventually* we'd save enough money to redo the bathrooms, kitchen, and floors, right? Love makes it possible to explain away any drawbacks. I was in love and nothing, *nothing* would stop me from living happily ever after in the house of my dreams.

BIG HOME-BUYING MISTAKE #2

Dan and I decided to bid on the town house. Since we didn't use a buyer's agent, the seller's Realtor emailed us a standard offer letter to use for our bid. Lucky for us, I was a law student at the time—a law student with a *real-life contract* in her hands. It was time to show the world what I could do. I rolled up my sleeves, pulled out a red pen, and got to work . . . on the standardized real estate offer letter used by millions of home buyers and sellers nationwide.

All crafty scams and loopholes *narrowly* avoided, I tried not to grin as I returned the completed offer to the seller's agent two days later. (Was it with a flourish? I can't remember.) I had no doubt she was impressed . . . right up until the minute she told us to take a hike.

At first, we couldn't believe it. We had made a good offer. But we ignored a critical fact: real estate transactions aren't only about the money. Thus I learned that some sellers are willing to walk away from a deal if the buyers are too much of a pain.

In the end, we lost the house because of my overzealousness AND I was devastated because I had fallen in love. I should've remained emotionally detached until we finalized the deal, but instead, I was heartbroken.

Luckily, I was able to learn from these two mistakes. Contrast that experience with our next one: A few Saturdays later, Dan and I went to a "For Sale by Owner" open house. We met the nice couple who owned the town home. We admired the three bedrooms, the outdoor courtyard, the basement-with-tremendous-potential. The neighborhood was great. We liked the town house a lot. Not loved. Just liked. A lot. (See what I did there?) After talking it over at a coffee shop around the corner, Dan and I decided to make an offer.

"Using a buyer's agent?" the sellers asked. Nope.

They invited us over for coffee the next morning. We brought the muffins.

The coffee was excellent. The blueberry muffins earned rave reviews.* Before the second round, we'd settled on a price.

How civilized. Every home deal should be like that one. In the end, the town house we bought was a much better fit for us.

First Two Lessons Learned

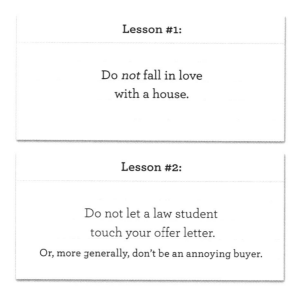

Lesson #1:

Do *not* fall in love
with a house.

Lesson #2:

Do not let a law student
touch your offer letter.

Or, more generally, don't be an annoying buyer.

Home buying is a nerve-wracking and emotional experience, and it's easy to forget that there's not one perfect dream

---

* See the appendix for the house-winning blueberry muffin recipe.

home for any of us out there. There are many. We shouldn't force it. You'll be a much better negotiator if you aren't head over heels in love with the place.

Fall in love with the deal, not just the house, because you make money when you buy the house, not when you sell it. When someone sells a house, she may list it at a market sale price, but it's unlikely the buyer will pay said list price. However, it is possible, as that buyer, to purchase a house far below the list price. In other words, you're more likely to get the $20,000 discount on the front end when you buy than to receive a bid that's $20,000 over the asking price when you sell. Of course, real estate tends to appreciate with time, but having patience for that good deal or to get your ideal home always works in your favor, which brings me to our biggest mistake of all.

BIG HOME-BUYING MISTAKE #3

After Dan finished his medical training, his most enticing job offer came from Knoxville, Tennessee. Although by now you know how the story ends, at the time we couldn't believe our good fortune. A new job, a new baby, a new life in a beautiful city with a mild climate and no state income tax—we'd hit the jackpot. Plus, we had saved enough money to buy a home that we could never dream of owning in Chicago: a brick colonial house on a hill with a screened-in, mosquito-free porch perfect for watching the sunset. Not once did we consider renting before buying.

Fast-forward one and a half years. We wanted out and the only thing stopping us was this house. On the plus side, Dan and I had learned from Lesson #1: we hadn't fallen *totally* in love with the house before we bought it. We made a successful lowball offer, which was key. Now that we needed to sell, we could list the house on the low side and not lose a lot of money. Unfortunately, the real estate market in those days was s-l-o-w; some of the other houses we had been considering were still on the market two years later.

During the six months that our Knoxville house was for sale, we had two showings. Two. Talk about stressful. We had already moved back to Chicago and were renting a place so that Dan could start his new job. Then, by some miracle and because the house was priced to sell, we found a buyer. We lost some money on the sale, but not as much as we would have lost had we paid the market value for the house. With the Knoxville sale behind us, we could now buy a home in Chicago from a favorable negotiating position—with no housing contingency and a flexible move-in date.

Lesson #3:

Rent (don't buy) if you're moving to a city you don't know well.

Here's where I beg you not to buy a house if you are new to a city. If you're moving to a city you don't know well, please rent first. Please. Pretty please. It will save you more time and stress than you can imagine if, for whatever reason, the house or neighborhood or job doesn't end up working. I know it's not fun to think about this current move not panning out, but you must. Not all moves are equal—buying a house in the town where you grew up is different than buying in a new city and state. So, if you plan to buy a house but you have uncertainty about the job, neighborhood, or place, just hear me out on this one.

Altogether, the costs of another potential relocation are higher than the costs of renting. Let's say you pay $250,000 for a house in St. Louis, Missouri, after you visited a couple of times. You move in and the neighborhood is fine, but you start to wish you'd bought a place closer to work. Then, a year later, a better job offer comes up in Kansas City and you want to take it. You list your house at $250,000 and get super lucky. A buyer pays full price with no contingencies and is ready to close whenever you are. Ideal scenario, right? Well, you will immediately lose $12,500 to your Realtor (assuming a 5 percent broker fee, though many charge 6 percent). That doesn't include any of the additional closing or transactional costs (let's say $1,000) or the property taxes (roughly $3,000). Could you have rented for less than $1,375 per month?

It's optimistic to think you could get the same price you originally paid so soon after buying your home. Buyers will assume you're a desperate seller, and you're more likely to get lowballed. Let's say you get $235,000 for your house instead. After broker fees, that's $223,250. Before any other costs associated with owning and selling the home (mortgage interest, maintenance, repairs, property taxes, remodeling, and so on), you're already down $26,750 in the year since you bought the place. That's serious money. What if the house "needs work" or fails the buyer's inspection, costing more time and money in repairs? *Buying a house when there's uncertainty about the job, neighborhood, or schools can be a costly mistake.* It's also a huge hassle to deal with a real estate transaction if you need to move again.

DOs BEFORE BUYING A HOUSE

From three home purchases in six years, we got a crash course in home buying. I've shared our three biggest mistakes as buyers, but I'm proud to say we did a few things right. Here are eleven tips for buying your first home.

1. Get your finances in order.

You should have money for a down payment, a steady paycheck, and a decent credit score before you buy a house. Dan and I prefer to avoid large risks when it comes to major financial decisions, so the numbers I present here may seem overly cautious to some people. Save enough money to put 20 percent down on your house. So, if you are purchasing a $300,000 home, you need $60,000 in cash to pay up front. You'll also need to save additional money for transactional costs. Let's say another $3,000.* The bank requires a payroll stub to show that you're currently employed, so now is *not* the time to quit your

---

* This money is to pay for an attorney, a home inspector, and other miscellaneous transaction costs.

job. You can improve your debt-to-income ratio by increasing regular payments toward outstanding debts. Finally, check your credit (FICO) score.* If you have issues on your credit report, try to fix those problems *before* you apply for a mortgage.†

2. Get preapproved for a mortgage.

Find out how much house the bank thinks you can afford. This will help you focus your house search. Also, your Realtor can use the preapproval letter to demonstrate that you're a serious and qualified buyer when you put in your first offer. Shop around to different mortgage companies or consider using a mortgage broker to get the best interest rates.

3. Research homes online.

Now that you know how much house you can afford, let the house-hunting obsession begin. Create alerts, save your favorite listings, and spend time surfing to your heart's content.

4. Make your Dream Home list.

Once you've seen what's out there, you should create a Dream Home list. We'll go into more detail in chapter 11 but, basically,

---

* You can do this for free online at Credit Karma.

† If you typically pay your credit card bills on time, but you have an odd late fee, call your credit card company to see if they'll waive that fee for you. This can help improve your credit.

you'll use this list to figure out what house features you love. What would your dream home look like? Write it all down and remember that no dream is too crazy.

5. Protect your dreams when working with a Realtor.

There's an inherent conflict between Realtors and their clients. Realtors want the quickest sale at a decent price. Buyers want their dream home at the ideal price and they may be willing to wait for it. As a home buyer, *you* need to protect your dreams. One solution is to put those Dream Home items on your must-have list, so that you get the number of bedrooms you need *and* the outdoor garden space you desire. Shop with your list in hand, because a charming fireplace may distract you from the thing you *really* want—like the ideal tree in your backyard to build your kids a treehouse (aka Dan's dream: accomplished) or that ocean view (aka my dream: still working on it).

6. Hire a Realtor.

Dan and I like shopping for homes on our own, but I wouldn't necessarily recommend that approach. In our experience, seller's agents do *not* like working with home buyers who are not represented by a Realtor (and those agents didn't even know me in my red pen days!). The standard practice is to hire a real estate agent. To find a good one, ask for recommendations from family or friends who live in the area or your new employer. Check out the appendix for a list of questions to ask a Realtor before you decide which one to hire.

7. Consider the school district, even if you don't have kids.

When Dan and I bought our first town house in Chicago, we bought the house for the walkable neighborhood and the space. We never considered the school district. We were pregnant with our first child at the time, and elementary school seemed a lifetime away. Less than four years later, we had three educations to worry about and a home to sell. Fortunately for us, we had lucked into buying a home in a top school district, so the sale happened quickly. Even if you don't have kids, consider the school district because it will impact your resale value. Top schools translate to better resale potential.

8. Find a quality home inspector.

The first time we bought a house, we hired a mediocre home inspector. He came to the house, checked off some boxes, and told us the place looked good. Several months after we bought our home, Dan and I went away for a weekend. When we came home, a stench engulfed us. Gas. Lots of it. The gas company promptly shut off the gas and told us, "We can't turn it back on until you get someone to fix the problem."

I set up appointments with multiple plumbers, but no one showed up. I was eight months pregnant without access to a hot shower or the ability to make a home-cooked meal on our gas stove. A week later and after I made a tearful phone call, a plumber had mercy on this emotional pregnant lady and showed up for the appointment. He repaired the eight (!) gas leaks in our home and it wasn't a cheap fix. For our first home, Dan and I didn't think we could afford a more expensive home inspector. We learned our lesson—you get what you pay for.

For our third home purchase, we hired the best home inspector we could find.[*] Halfway through the home inspection, Tom turned to us and said, "There are so many problems with this house that I'd be happy to end the inspection now and I'll only charge you half." Since I really liked the house, we asked him to finish. He continued the inspection and found even more electrical, plumbing, and structural problems—not to mention the rats. Dan and I walked away from a house that I thought was going to be our forever home. It was the best decision we've ever made.

9. Hire a lawyer.

Buying a house is the biggest financial investment you'll make in your lifetime. Hire a lawyer to protect that investment. This preemptive measure will cost you a few hundred dollars but can save you thousands if there turns out to be a problem on your title[†] or any other issue when you sell your home later.

[*] We also binge-watched HGTV's *Holmes on Homes* and *Holmes Inspection*. Our time spent watching these shows, coupled with a quality home inspector, saved us from financial ruin.

[†] The title is a bundle of rights in the property. The deed is the legal document that transfers home ownership from seller to buyer. If there are any problems with the title, this can be a problem for you as the buyer. Problems could include judgments, liens, or bankruptcies that affect the property. Too much legalese? This is what lawyers are for.

10. Make an offer that makes you happy.

I like to make lowball offers, although this isn't possible in every real estate market. For markets like Silicon Valley or Seattle, figure out how high you would be willing to go for your budget and for your happiness. Just because you can afford a higher price doesn't mean you'll be happy paying it. In a buyer's market, make low offers. You can always negotiate to a higher price. You can also negotiate details like contingencies and the closing date. If you're flexible on the closing date, let the seller know. If possible, don't waive the contingencies because they are there to protect you. *Just remember that if this house doesn't work out, there will be another home out there for you.*

11. Be kind.

Real estate is a relationship business. Being kind doesn't mean paying full price if the market dictates a lower price. However, it does mean being reasonable in your interactions with the sellers and the agents. Don't fuss over details that don't mean that much to you—whether it's the closing date or if the sellers leave the chandelier—and, I don't know, maybe don't mark up and edit a standard offer letter. Treat the other side as if you were colleagues. Be respectful. Also, remember that the sellers' neighbors will soon be your neighbors and they'll probably hear how the deal went down.

One minute you're buying a house, the next it's time to sell. To find out how to sell a house, read on for tips on staging and maintaining your sanity. If you still can't decide whether to rent or buy, the next chapter may persuade you. It's like babysitting your sister's kids when you're deciding whether to take the plunge into parenthood. It'll make you think twice.

4

HOW TO SELL YOUR HOUSE WITHOUT KILLING ANYONE FIRST

So bitter is it [selling a house while moving], death is little more.

—DANTE ALIGHIERI, *Inferno*
(Brackets added, but I know that's what he meant.)

Italy, 1308 A.D.: Just as Dante finishes tidying the living quarters, his sons scatter Crusades action figures across the floor. Outside, the potential buyer lifts the door knocker and strikes the plate thrice. She crosses her arms and taps her foot as she waits for the door to open. Never mind that she's ten minutes early for the showing. Dante can't take it anymore. He grabs his quill pen, channels that unmistakable home-seller feeling, and starts to write *Inferno*. So, he has that going for him. This is pure conjecture, of course, but I'm pretty sure that's how *The Divine Comedy* was born.

For the rest of us, selling a house in the midst of a move is simply a circle of hell we can't avoid. If you own a house and you're moving, you probably need to sell your house first. Here's how to do it without losing your mind.

DECLUTTER AS SOON AS POSSIBLE

We'll cover *how* to declutter in the next chapter, but know that decluttering is critical to both Happy Moving and happy home selling. Be aggressive. Get rid of everything you can and don't worry about your place looking too sparse. It won't. The less furniture and fewer dishes you have, the more spacious your home will look. Besides, it's much easier to tuck away two items instead of twenty when you do a last-minute sweep before a showing. The secret to happy home selling is a decluttered home that requires minimal maintenance between showings.

WOO BUYERS AT EACH STEP

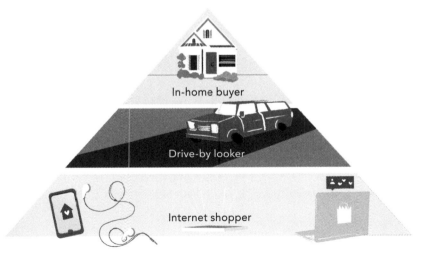

In-home buyer

Drive-by looker

Internet shopper

Your first challenge is to attract the internet shopper. To do that, you need beautiful photos, curb appeal, and a staged home. Professional, bright, and staged photos will get buyers to save your house to their "favorites" in the online listings. An enticing home description can also help and this is one place where adjectives don't hurt: "sunny," "charming," "cozy" are all your friends when writing copy. Step one complete.

If a prospective buyer likes the sound of your place, the next thing they'll do is drive by your house. Landscaping and curb appeal are critical—good landscaping can increase your expected sale price by up to 20 percent. If your house doesn't pass the drive-by test, you won't get a call for a showing.

To lure the buyer, you want to sell an *extraordinary lifestyle*. Your home should be aspirational. The buyer shouldn't think about the work that comes with the house. You don't want to remind people that they need to take out the trash, rake the leaves, or pick up litter that blows in from the alley. Instead, your buyer should imagine sipping lemonade in the shade on the porch while reading a book. Because, you know, that's what everyone does after work on a Monday night, right? Sure, they don't have time for that now, but maybe if they lived *in your home* . . .

Quick Fixes to Improve Curb Appeal for That Drive-By Shopper

- Clear away outdoor clutter. This includes toys, rakes, garbage cans, snow shovels, salt bags, and leftover mulch.
- Put away home security signs, "Beware of Dog" signs, and so forth.

- Purchase a new welcome mat, and clean or replace house numbers.
- Clean your mailbox. If it's worn out or kitschy,* replace it.
- Add potted plants by your front door. Symmetry is appealing.
- Add landscape lighting.
- Depending on your time and budget, consider repainting your home's exterior, replacing the windows, or doing more extensive landscaping.

Fabulous! A potential buyer booked a showing. Now let's get the inside ready.

STAGE YOUR HOUSE FOR A QUICK SALE

According to the Real Estate Staging Association, staged houses sell 90 percent faster. Even if the percentage were half that, it would be worth your time to make a few changes. What is home staging? It's prepping your home so that it appeals to a wide range of potential buyers. Think model apartment or Pottery Barn catalog, not Lady Gaga's pied-à-terre (unless you are Lady Gaga, in which case, carry on). Neutral sells. It's also time to take down those family photos and personal mementos. You want the buyer to imagine herself in the home, living the life *she's* always dreamed of. She shouldn't be thinking about the life *you're* currently living.

---

* There is a time and a place for manatee mailboxes, and this is not it. Super adorable? Um, totally. Appealing to a wide array of buyers? Not so much

You can go in a few directions with home staging. One option is to ask a home-staging company to create a detailed report for your home. This will set you back several hundred dollars, but you'll get a staging checklist made just for you. You can then use this professional advice to incorporate the changes on your own. For an additional fee, the company can make the changes for you. The other option is to handle the job yourself with advice you'll find in this chapter.

HOT TIP:
Ask potential Realtors if a detailed staging report is included in their marketing budget (which means it's free for you). More than half of real estate agents provide some form of staging services, so consider this when you choose your Realtor.

To go the DIY route, let's first figure out your home-staging goals.

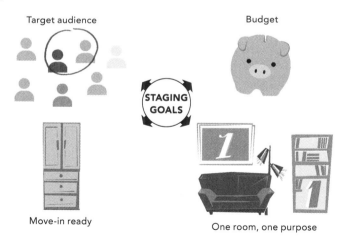

Target audience

Budget

STAGING GOALS

Move-in ready

One room, one purpose

Before you make any changes, think about your target audience. Who wants to buy your studio apartment in a six-floor walk-up or your four-bedroom house in the suburbs? Your home will not appeal to everyone, so focus your energy on the people who will be most interested. A good way to figure out your target audience is to think about who *you* were when you bought your home. Appeal to the person you were at that moment in time. This will help you decide whether to make the back room an office or a nursery. If you're staging on your own, ask a person in your target demographic to do a walk-through. So, instead of asking your mom's opinion on what to change in your one-bedroom condo, ask your newly married friend for some honest feedback.

Next, make a budget. How much are you willing to spend to increase the value of your home? What improvements can you make to get your home sold quickly and at the best price? If your funds are limited, you'll want to focus on decluttering, painting, and brightening your space.

Your goal for your home is to make it move-in ready so buyers think, "Wow! I don't need to do a thing." With your budget in hand, you can start to make some changes. According to the National Association of Realtors, this is the order you want to tackle your staging goals: living room, kitchen, master bedroom, dining room, bathroom, children's bedrooms, and guest bedroom.

Maximize your space and your resources by giving each room one and only one purpose. If your guest room is currently also an office and a play space, choose one identity for the room when you stage it. If something doesn't fit with that purpose, move it out of the room. Maybe your sister would be willing to temporarily store your furniture in her attic or you might consider renting a storage unit.

Now that you know your staging goals, it's time to focus on selling a lifestyle to the home buyers. You want to create a clean, bright, well-maintained home that makes the buyer dream of the type of person she wants to be.

• Deep clean home.
• Declutter.
• Remove large furniture pieces.
• Display items by 3s.
• Store clutter.

• Add fresh coat of paint.
• Remove heavy draperies or dark rugs.
• Use white towels and linens.
• Improve lighting.

Clean

Bright

LIVING THE LIFE

Well-maintained

Aspirational

• Make minor home repairs.
• Mow lawn.
• Trim trees.

• Get hygge with it.
• Remove any signs of "work."
• Highlight the architectural features.
• Inspire dreams.

Become a home-cleaning rock star

The home-selling limbo stage is a weird one. You feel like you're living someone else's life, or at least I did. Toilets scrubbed on a daily basis, countertops sparkling after every meal, toys constantly organized and in their place—one in, one out. It can be exhausting, but it can also make you feel like a rock star. This may not be the life you live forever, but you can do it for a few months. Anything is possible for a few months.

To keep a house clean, you need a good starting point. So, declutter with purpose. After you take your house photos for your listing, maintain that level of cleanliness. That means making your bed every morning as soon as you wake up. Do a two-second wipe down of the bathroom counter after you brush your teeth. Hang up your coat when you get home from work. Make meals that provide easy leftovers or eat out more often than you usually do. Tidy as you go throughout the day and spend twenty minutes each evening to clean up any clutter. Also, keep empty storage bins on hand. They're useful for those last-minute sweeps when you get a call for an impromptu showing.

Make necessary home repairs

Unfinished home repairs are like roaches. For every one a buyer sees, she knows there are hundreds more lurking behind walls and strategically placed potted plants. Take the time to fix the broken light switch plates, the hole in the laundry room wall, or the faulty door handle. Magic Eraser can wipe away unsightly scuffs in the hallway. For large home repairs, you may prefer to give the buyer a credit so you don't need to deal with a roof replacement while getting ready to move. In other words, you can give the buyer an agreed-upon dollar amount so she can make the repair after the home sale instead of fixing it yourself.

Store large or unnecessary items elsewhere

You want to create good flow when buyers come to your house. Obtrusive furniture or large television sets can be jarring. Ideally, you would store your big TV. This is especially true if your TV is an older model since this makes your entire home feel dated. For the rest of your furniture, notice when a friend comes to your house. Can she easily walk from one room to another or does she stop to navigate around certain pieces? Consider renting a storage unit or asking a family member to store a few items. Also, your garage is *not* a substitute for a storage facility, because your garage is part of the usable home space that you want to show to buyers.

Lighten and brighten your space

A fresh coat of paint is the difference between passing out in your sweatpants after a rough night and getting decked out in that red dress after a visit to the salon. There's no comparison. If you want to keep your costs down on this makeover story, use one coat of paint and one color throughout the house. Color trends change, so play it safe by using a neutral paint color like beige, creamy white, or pale gray. Then, dress up your home in white. Here are more ways to brighten and lighten your space:

- Add table lamps for cozy lighting.
- Use light bulbs with 800 to 1,000 lumens for staging purposes.
- Buy some inexpensive white towels and a white duvet cover to use as display linens.
- Roll up and store dark rugs.
- Remove heavy drapery or curtains to let in sunlight.
- Remove dark fireplace grates and place LED candles in the fireplace.

Neutralize your space to make room for the buyer's dream

Why is it so important to neutralize a space? It's because you're selling the home buyer on *his* dream, not yours. So, it's time to put away the photos of that fishing trip in Florida or your wall of White Sox memorabilia. Pack your kitchen magnets, your family's artwork, and that sign that says "Mind your own biscuits and life will be gravy." That's not to say that your home should lack warmth or beauty. You just want the buyer to focus on the selling points of the house itself, like the original crown molding, the energy-efficient windows, or the forest view.

Remove items that remind buyers of housework

You want to convince the buyer that your house is well-behaved at all times. It's like the smiling, happy kids in everyone's Facebook posts. You know there must be tantrums, but you forget this when you're scrolling through the cheerful feeds. Get your home in order so it seems picture-perfect.

- Don't leave the plunger next to the toilet.
- Avoid cleaning products with strong chemical smells.
- Avoid using scented products, incense, oils, air fresheners, and perfumes.
- Put away rodent traps or wasp repellants.
- Keep countertops clear.
- Store small kitchen appliances like toasters, coffee makers, and blenders.
- Pack up your linens if you don't have a linen closet.
- Straighten pictures, rugs, and towels.
- Clean out your front closet, since it's often the first door a buyer will open.
- Place a large welcome mat in your entry area.*

* When buyers walk into your house, they will stand on your indoor mat until they decide whether to take off their shoes. Make sure the welcome mat is large enough that they don't feel stuck on a tiny island. You want to promote a feeling of spacious living.

Get *hygge* with it (pronounced "HOO-ga," unless you're trying to rhyme with Will Smith)

All work and no play never turns out well. The same is true when it comes to home staging and home selling. Yes, you need neutral, but you also want cozy and happy. This is still your home. You should enjoy your last few months together. Hygge can help you do that.

If you haven't heard about hygge, it's a Danish concept that's tough to translate. Some say it means "cozy" living, but Danes would shake their heads and say it's so much more than that. So, let's defer to the expert. In *The Little Book of Hygge: Danish Secrets to Happy Living,* Meik Wiking describes hygge:

> Hygge is about an atmosphere and an experience, rather than about things. It is about being with the people we love. A feeling of home. . . . Hygge is about giving yourself and others a treat. It is about savoring the moment and the simple pleasures of good food and good company.[*]

To incorporate hygge and a modicum of sanity into your life while your house is for sale, do the following:

---

* Meik Wiking, *The Little Book of Hygge: Danish Secrets to Happy Living* (New York: William Morrow, 2017), pp. iv, 215.

Bake cookies
Make a meal at home
Turn down the lights
Light candles
Wear fuzzy socks
Eat chocolate
Use a soft throw
Put on some music
Invite friends over
Sit and breathe

Ahhh. I feel so much better just thinking about that. Give yourself a minute for hygge. When you're ready, let's move on to my favorite moving topic ... decluttering. It's the reason moving was invented.

5

___

THE SECRET TO HAPPY MOVING

Get Rid of Everything You Own

*Why did I save all those clothes? I felt like that guy with
amnesia from* Memento. *I'd pick up a pair of stirrup pants
and an image would flash into my head: me standing in
front of a mirror thinking, "These are really slimming."
Then all memories of that outfit and time would
disappear.* —ELLEN DEGENERES, *The Funny Thing Is...*

For the record, I'm not a minimalist. I'm your average mom
with three kids, living in a suburban home full of closets. With
kids involved in after-school activities, a husband who loves
to build outdoor projects, and my own occasional urges to
update the old wardrobe, it doesn't take long for possessions
to accumulate. However, I learned from our many moves that
the simplification of our belongings can lead to a happier and
less chaotic home. If you want to save yourself a few moving
headaches, then free yourself of the items that you no longer
need. In this chapter, I'll guide you through how to declutter
for your move. I also hope to encourage you to make a regular
habit of it, long after the moving boxes are gone.

More than once I've heard, "Oh, you're so lucky you're moving. I wish I had a reason to clean out my house." So, let's just

stop for a moment and consider how fortunate you are. Wow, you lucky mover, you. (Seriously, though, moving *is* a blessing in disguise—albeit an elaborate disguise.) Now that you've reveled in your good fortune for a moment, let's break down the decluttering process into small steps. First, refer to the chart below for an overview.

HOW TO START DECLUTTERING

WHO:	You (+ someone else?)
WHAT:	Pick a category. Let's start with books.
WHEN:	Pick a time. How about Saturday morning?
WHERE:	The place where most items in that category live.
WHY:	Pick the reason that resonates most—save money, make money, help others, continued usefulness of item.
HOW:	By category. One day at a time.

Now that we have the basics, let's cover the six rules for decluttering for a move:

1. IF YOU'RE A KEEPER INSTEAD OF A DECLUTTERER, ASK FOR HELP.

Some of us can't let go of our possessions (the Keepers) while some of us can't wait to fill the car with bags of Goodwill donations (the Declutterers). If you fall into the Keeper category, you may need to ask for help from a Declutterer friend. She can give you the emotional support you need when it's time to decide what items will make the move with you.

A QUICK SELF-EVALUATION TO FIGURE OUT IF YOU NEED A HELPER

Please answer the following questions so you can evaluate your Keeper tendencies.

1. **As you prepare to pack your dining table, you see:**

    a. Rosy visions of your loved ones passing around the Caesar salad and telling funny stories.
    b. A wooden table that's 78 inches by 40 inches and six chairs in good condition.

2. **You open the cabinet under your bathroom sink and:**

    a. Feel gratitude that you've held on to those free samples—you might need them one day.
    b. Grab the closest trash can.

3. You lay out your sweaters on the bed to start packing and:

   a. Know you'll get *so* much more use out of them next winter.
   b. Put all but two sweaters in the donation pile.

Are you a Keeper or a Declutterer?

If you answered all Bs, you're a Declutterer. Please proceed to discard your items without further ado. If you answered all As, you're a Keeper, and you'll want to ask a Declutterer friend or family member for help. I know it can be hard to let go of that futon you've had since freshman year of college, but there's a payoff, I promise.

2. MAKE TIME TO DECLUTTER.

When's the best time to declutter? Now, tonight, after you get the audio version of this book so you can pack while you listen. If tonight doesn't work, decide on a time that *does* work. *The "When" should be as soon as possible.* Put it on your calendar if that's what works for you. Tell your mom that you plan to pack on Saturday so she can harass you about it. Post a shot of you packing the dishes on Instagram to garner sympathy and feel accountable to your friends. Accountability can be a great motivator.

3. START WITH THE HEAVY ITEMS IN YOUR HOME.

Decluttering for a move is a little different than decluttering to "spark joy." When you move, you need to consider if you want to keep large and heavy items because weight and size matter. One part of the equation is: How much do I love the item? The other part is: Is it better to sell or donate this item instead of packing it, moving it, and unpacking it?

When Dan and I moved from Columbus, Ohio, to Palo Alto, California, our apartment size went from 1,200 square feet to 375 square feet. We chose to sell our leather recliner because (a) it wouldn't fit in our California apartment and (b) moving and storing it would cost more than selling it and replacing it if needed. (In case you're wondering, we never replaced our leather recliner.) On the other hand, we chose to keep our lift-top coffee table that doubled as our dining table because we loved that piece of furniture and it worked well in our little apartment.

So, you want to consider what items you love, but you also want to think about what you can use in your new space and how much hassle and money it will cost you to get your belongings there. I suggest the following decluttering order based on weight, ease of decluttering, and ability to sell the items.

Decluttering Order for Moving

1. Books
2. Magazines
3. Furniture
4. Sports equipment

5. Shoes
6. Clothes
7. Kitchen appliances
8. Dishware

9. Decorative accessories
10. Toiletries
11. Toys
12. Paperwork

4. CREATE FIVE PILES.

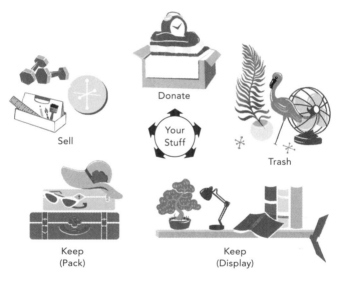

Donate

Your Stuff

Sell

Trash

Keep
(Pack)

Keep
(Display)

To decide what to purge, the question you should ask yourself is: "What do I want to keep?" The question is *not*: "What do I need to toss?" With that in mind, write "Keep" and "Sell" on two pieces of paper and tape the signs to two empty boxes to help you manage the separate piles. Then, grab several garbage bags and make "Trash" and "Donate" labels for them.

Go through your items and as soon as you finish a decluttering session, take out the trash to make room to pack the remaining "Keep" items. For donations, itemize each object before bagging, then put the bags into your car right away so they're ready to be taken to a donation site. (Later in the chapter I'll give you more details about itemizing donations for tax purposes.) Schedule a pickup with a charitable organization for large donation items, but realize this can take two to three weeks. For items you plan to sell, take photos and put those items aside. Also, set aside "Keep" items you choose to display for the time being (either because you plan to sell your house or because it's too soon to pack your coffee maker).

5. LAY OUT EVERY SINGLE ITEM IN THE CATEGORY.

In order to maximize the efficiency of this decluttering process, you don't want to declutter room by room. Instead, like organizing consultant Marie Kondo advises, declutter by category. Here's what you do so you can get rid of as much stuff as possible: Gather items from the same category and put them all in one place. Lay the items out together and examine them. This way, you'll notice if there's overlap or if there are items you don't want now that you can see how many of that particular item you own. You get a free pass *only* on the furniture category since I would never ask you to squeeze all your furniture into one room to review it. That might be a bit much.

Let's say you are decluttering your T-shirts. *Choose a place where you can display each and every T-shirt you own.* Every. Single. T-shirt. Grab your T-shirts from your bedroom, your living room, your office, and your gym bag. After you lay out the T-shirts, you may find that you have six that you don't really like or two that look identical. If you gathered thirty T-shirts from around your house, you might find that you wear only three or four of them. Seeing everything together at once clarifies how much you need—and how much you don't.

For us, the book category is a tough one. My husband and I both love to read and must force ourselves to ask if we really need to keep *everything.* Not every single book I own brings me the same level of happiness. *Civil Procedure: Theory and Practice,* for one, doesn't make me smile . . . even a little. Yet, for some reason, I lugged it across the country more than once, long after I finished law school. It did finally occur to me that I'd never, ever revisit the rules of civil procedure for a few good laughs or for old times' sake. So, we sold this and other textbooks and donated the rest. We pocketed some cash and shaved easy pounds off the moving load.

6. DECIDE WHY DECLUTTERING IS IMPORTANT TO YOU.

When you declutter for a move, it's not only about finding the items that spark joy—which can be an important distinction if you're the kind of person who doesn't think "declutter" and "joy" should appear in the same sentence. This is about simplifying your home to reduce your stress level, save you time down the road, and best prepare you to set up your new, happy space. If that isn't motivation enough, you can also help others and make or save money.

WHY I WANT TO DECLUTTER BEFORE MY MOVE

Make Money
Garage sale
Tax deductions

Help Others
Give a coat
to someone
who needs one

Save Money
Less spent on movers
or bigger truck

Items Remain Useful
Books can be enjoyed by another reader

Most of the reasons for decluttering before you move are self-explanatory. You will save money if you don't move unnecessary items. It feels good when you know your unused coat can help keep someone warm or when your book lives a second life when someone else reads it. How to make money when you declutter the objects in your home can be a little more complex.

To make money when you declutter, you have three options: (1) sell in person, (2) sell online, or (3) receive a tax deduction for itemized donations. I've done them all and there are pros and cons to each. If you decide to go the online or garage sale route, you need to plan early because items might not sell right away and you don't want to move things you no longer want. Also, remember to take pictures of your couch that is for sale before your home is a mess from packing.

When it comes to donations, *many people often miss one major step.* To optimize the tax impact of your donation, you must itemize every article of clothing, each book, each wineglass. We used to write "three bags of clothes" until we realized how much money we could've deducted on our tax return. Take a look at the Donation Value Guide in the appendix. If you donate two pairs of women's pants, two blouses, two sweaters, and two dresses, you can deduct between $34 and $224 for these eight items alone.[*]

Whatever decluttering reason motivates you, keep it in mind while you get the work done. Then, after you have decluttered by category, it's time to start packing. All you need to do now is put the items you love into a moving box. And the greatest joy is yet to come: the moment when you unpack that box in your new home. Inside you'll find items you love, items you need, and none of the clutter you had back at the old place. Unpacking just got a whole lot easier. Well done, you.

---

[*] The value depends on the age and condition of the items, and deductions apply for those who itemize their deductions. Consult your tax professional for more detailed advice.

A QUICK WORD ON DECLUTTERING WITH KIDS

I put toys toward the bottom of the decluttering list because oftentimes we contemplate a move long before we are able to tell the kids about it. If the time is right for you, declutter toys now but with your child's buy-in.

Only you fully know your child's needs, so let those needs take priority. Some children may cling to everyday objects during an emotional time like moving. That broken light-up ring your daughter received as a party favor two years ago may suddenly become her prized possession. If there are items that seem too difficult for your child to part with right now but that you know should probably be thrown away, consider packing these toys together in their own box, separate from the rest of the toys. When you arrive at your new home, don't rush to unpack the boxes filled with toys that seemed important to your child only during the decluttering phase. Wait a few months, let the family settle in a bit, and then decide how to proceed.

To make decluttering a fun and entertaining family event, you may want to try out my Toy Store Method on page 66. Every year my family celebrates Donation Weekend on the weekend after Halloween, so I have plenty of ~~bribes~~ candy incentives for the kids. I clear off the basement floor and gather every toy we own from around the house. Then I separate the toys into categories so that the basement looks like an official toy store: dolls, puzzles, board games, trucks, doll houses, imaginary play setups, stuffed animals, and Legos.

ALI'S TOY STORE METHOD

WHO:	The kids
WHAT:	Toys
WHEN:	Weekend after Halloween
WHERE:	Basement
WHY:	Help others, make money, item remains useful
HOW:	Read on . . .

My kids, Victoria, Joseph, and Charlotte, each receive a different-colored pad of sticky notes. The toy store doors open (my arm lifts) and the kids race to "buy" everything they want. To buy a toy, they slap a sticky note on it. At first my kids buy everything, and they place a note on every Star Wars Lego or mosaic set they see. Soon (thankfully) they begin to lose steam. The sticky notes don't fly as fast and their attention fades. By the end, piles of toys remain untouched. You've had a good run, Elmo, but there's another kid waiting to love you.

My kids sometimes get "donator's regret" as I like to call it, so I set aside the "purchased" toys and invite the kids back for another round. Then everyone sleeps on it, and I do a final closeout sale the next morning so everyone has enough time to think about it overnight. There always seems to be one item that a kid decides she can't live without, which is fine. The next morning, she puts a sticker on the toy and it moves back into the keeper pile.

The reason the kids love Donation Weekend is that we make it fun and silly. Trumpets blare for the grand opening, the closing ritual is done with a British accent (because everyone knows that's fancier), and there might be a pile of Reese's Peanut Butter Cups by the register. Plus, reframing the question has been key in helping the kids feel good about donating their toys or books. We don't ask our kids: "What do you want to get rid of?" We do ask them: "What do you want to keep?"

When you declutter your items, reframe the question. It will help you feel better about what you keep and what you toss. *Choose what you want to move instead of what you will leave behind.*

If you're worried about how the move will impact your kids, continue to the next page.

If you're not moving with kids, but you'd like a quick rundown of what you need to do before you move, jump over to chapter 7.

If you prefer *Choose Your Own Adventure* books where you end up in a pit of lava, go run a hot bath.

6

BUILDING YOUR CHILD'S RESILIENCE—SHE'LL THANK YOU LATER

The way I see it, if you want the rainbow, you gotta put up with the rain.   —DOLLY PARTON

We don't give kids today enough credit. In my day, parents would take their children for long drives along curvy roads without strapping them in the back seat. We kids would curl into balls and see how far we could roll without falling off. The last one on the bench seat would chug a victory Pixie Stix, and then we'd start a new round. I know what you're thinking, and yes, we still had a lot to learn in the eighties, but there is a teeny sliver of wisdom in there.

While I would never let anyone ride in my car without wearing a seat belt today, there's something to be said for having faith that our kids will be able to handle life's curves. Our kids can succeed regardless of (and often in spite of) our actions. As parents, we need to provide guidance—but at the same time, we need to show our kids that we believe that they can handle a difficult situation, that they will become more resilient *because* of the hiccups in life. Moving gives your family an opportunity to help build that resilience. Accept this gift for what it is.

Once you've decided that moving can be a great thing for your child, you can be a helpful resource for him. You just need to recognize what moving means to a kid. As adults, we understand the basic logistics of moving. You pack up your stuff, move it to a new place, unpack when you get there, and get on with your life. On the surface it seems straight-forward. However, if this is your child's first time moving, don't assume he understands anything about what's going to happen.

Take six-year-old Max, for example. His parents bought a new house only ten minutes away from their current place. When Max's mother, Jessica, shared the good news with her son, she didn't anticipate much trouble since the house was just one neighborhood over. Days later she found Max sob-bing in his room. Alarmed, she asked him what was wrong. He looked up at her with red, swollen eyes: "Do we need to leave Louie here . . . or will he live in a kennel?"

Poor Max. Max saw bags of unwanted clothes stuffed in the trunk on their way to Goodwill. He witnessed his parents wav-ing dismissively at their belongings: "Let's just leave the cur-tains and chandelier behind for the new owners." Naturally, Max became alarmed that there might also be consequences for their dog, Louie.

Sometimes adults lose track of a child's perspective. It's easy to get caught up in the whirlwind of moving, and we for-get how it might appear to a child. Let's consider some ways to reduce your child's fears and better incorporate his needs into this major family event.

> ### 5 Ways to Help Your Child Through a Move
>
> 1. Have "the moving talk" as soon as possible.
> 2. Explain how life will be the same or different after the move.
> 3. Give your child a sense of control.
> 4. Be optimistic about the move and share that feeling with your child.
> 5. Recognize that some sadness is natural.

1. HAVE "THE MOVING TALK" AS SOON AS POSSIBLE.

When Jack and Sarah decided to move to Portland to be closer to Sarah's family, they both needed to find jobs. It took a while, but they finally landed the perfect gigs. With that piece squared away, they were ready. Sarah and Jack planned a chocolate chip pancake breakfast (their kids' favorite) on a Sunday morning to break the news. But first, they enjoyed a night out with friends at their weekly Saturday barbecue.

Jack's best friend, Aaron, slapped Jack on the shoulder and said, "I can't believe you and Sarah are moving." They heard a yelp behind them that sounded like someone had stepped on a cat. Jack and Aaron turned around to see eight-year-old Lyla staring up at her dad, mouth open, enormous tears falling at rocket speed: "We're moving?!"

Not ideal, it's true. But these things happen.

In a perfect world, your child would be the first to hear

about the move—from you. Even if sharing the news doesn't go exactly as planned, I have some tips to help you through "the moving talk."

First, find a time and place to chat where you can be a patient parent, an active listener, and a good hugger. Then, focus on the four Ws:

- *Why* are you moving?
- *Where* are you moving?
- *When* are you moving?
- *What three things* make this move exciting?

Here's a script for you:

Kids, please come into the living room. Mom and I have something to share. Mommy got an amazing job in Denver, Colorado. Her job starts in January, so we'll be moving to Colorado sometime after the holidays. You guys will love it because:

1. We'll be closer to Grandma and Grandpa;

2. Our backyard will have big trees so we can put up a zip line; and

3. We'll be near the mountains so we can go snow tubing.

It's going to be an incredible adventure for our family.

The reality is that you'll get to the "so we'll be moving to Colorado" part and the tears will begin (sorry, but that's the likely scenario). Still, keep those three reasons to be happy about the move handy. Why only three? Research shows that we are happier if we focus on three reasons to be grateful instead of a larger number. As an example, you might be happy about your move because you'll be close to extended family, in a safer neighborhood, and only steps away from an ice cream shop. If you try to write down thirteen reasons why you're grateful, however, you might struggle to come up with that thirteenth reason and you'll begin to think, "Maybe I'm not so happy after all" or "Am I really moving because there's a famous opera house an hour away?"

Keep the talk short and simple. Be ready for questions and answer them to the best of your ability. If you're unsure about the timing or the logistics, just be honest. After you share the basic information ("We're moving"), let your child lead the discussion.

Also, beware when your kid asks for a pet. Kids have a sixth sense about the situation at hand. They can detect your weakness, and they're ready to strike the moment you put moving on the table. It's fine to use a kitty to sweeten the pot if you've planned for that in advance. But don't make a decade-long commitment without some forethought.

You'll want to keep the lines of communication open after the official talk, too. Use dinnertime or bedtime to discuss any follow-up questions your child may have. You could also try journaling with your child. In my house, my kids write in their parent-child journal before bed and then leave the journal outside their bedroom door. I'll read the entries, write a response, and then return the journals for each child to find in the morning. We might draw pictures or write about our day or start a multiday game of tic-tac-toe. It's up to the kids—they're the bosses.

You might find that while *your* thoughts are fully consumed by the move, your son is more focused on whether tomorrow's school lunch is turkey nachos or chili. (It's all about priorities.) Journaling can be a fun outlet for the two of you, and it gives your child a chance to open up about his concerns when the time feels right to him. The journal also gives you a way to communicate without the conversation being derailed by a text message or interrupted by a sibling. You can journal with kids of any age as long as your child is willing to try it.

2. EXPLAIN HOW LIFE WILL BE THE SAME OR DIFFERENT AFTER THE MOVE.

When your child faces a large number of life changes all at once, it can help to visualize the similarities and differences between your current life and your new one. A friend of mine created a PowerPoint presentation to get his four kids excited about their move from Chicago to Seattle. He showed them pictures of the Market Theater Gum Wall (equally disgusting *and* awesome), the first Starbucks (*oohs* and *aahs*), and the Space Needle ("Is that where we're going to live?"). The kids understood they would need to change schools and make new friends, but they worried about something else. Would they be able to continue their activities? My friend had anticipated this question, and he shared photos of the basketball team and the swimming facilities in Seattle.

An alternative would be to create a poster board with "Same" and "Different" columns during dinnertime or at a family meeting. Ask the kids to give ideas or to help draw on the board. Highlight the traditions you'll keep, like trick-or-treating or apple picking or making sugar cookies for the holidays. Talk about the differences, too, so that the kids know what to expect. Maybe your new house will be smaller than your current home because you're moving to a more expensive city. Maybe the kids will take the bus to school now instead of getting a ride from you. Create appropriate expectations to help reduce their fears.

3. GIVE YOUR CHILD A SENSE OF CONTROL.

One of the worst feelings for children who are moving is that they don't have any control over the situation. This can be especially true for teenagers, who are already struggling between wanting more independence and having to comply with parental rules. Return some control to your child to help relieve tension and to help everyone feel happy about the move.

Find age-appropriate decisions for your child to make. For a young child, this might mean deciding how to set up her room. Find three or four paint colors you'd be happy with and then let your child make the final decision. Sketch the blueprints for your child's bedroom on paper. Cut out scaled representations of the furniture and ask your child to try various arrangements for his room. A teen might help you decide on the best house for the family or the school district. Kids of all ages can be involved in decluttering, packing, and unpacking. When you arrive at your new home, let your child unpack his possessions however he wants so he can create a sanctuary for himself, a private space to get away when he needs a break.

During the move, give each member of the family one special box or bin for "critical items." I recommend see-through plastic bins, so that you can find any item on demand. These bins will be readily accessible and might travel in the family vehicle instead of the moving van. A young child might fill her bin with a special blanket, a stuffed animal, or a favorite book. Because the bin of personal treasures is always trackable, the child will feel more in control than if these items are buried in the depths of a truck trailer. Once you reach your destination, the quick access means essential items will be there right when you need them.

4. BE OPTIMISTIC ABOUT THE MOVE AND SHARE THAT FEELING WITH YOUR CHILD.

As difficult as it may be, especially if your child expresses her frustration with the move on a daily basis, *it's important to remain positive and to demonstrate optimism and enthusiasm.* Even when you're in the middle of packing your thousandth box, your child will look to you for clues on how to feel. Whatever your moving situation may be, do your best to keep the negative thoughts unspoken, especially around the children.

Children look to parents as role models. So, if you want your child to be happy about the move, you need to project happiness. Ice cream can help, too.

5. RECOGNIZE THAT SOME SADNESS IS NATURAL.

Moving can be exciting, but it's also a time of loss—both for those who are leaving and for those left behind. It's natural to feel sorrow. As much as we want to cheer up our kids, we also need to give them the time and space to mourn.

I remember bedtime being the hardest part of the day after we moved to Knoxville. I felt like we'd made a terrible mistake—not because of the city or the job or the house, but because my kids were so sad. The fact that my kids muffled their sobs made it even worse. They didn't want us to worry about them. But in the privacy of their own bedrooms, they'd cry and cry for the friends they'd left behind. (Insert mom-bawling emoji here.) There's no doubt that this part can be excruciating for you and for your kids, but it does get easier as the months go on.

You can help by recognizing that your child's way of mourning may not be through tears. She might act out or slam doors or make hurtful comments. As difficult as it may be, don't take this personally or blame your child. This is your child's way of making sense of a world that has been turned upside down. She may not know how to react to the situation. To guide her, empathize, give her a hug, and reassure her that the family will get through this together. Then, give her the time to mourn the loss of her old life.

STOP FEELING GUILTY—YOU'RE BUILDING RESILIENCE

The five tips for helping your child through a move are for her. This one is for you. If you feel guilty about moving the family, repeat this mantra: *"The kids will be fine."*

Kids are resilient. Kids move all the time. Almost seven million families move in the United States every year. And you know what? They're good. I can't say I've talked to *all* of them, but the people I *have* talked to—parents or adults who moved as kids—are happy, well-adjusted, and resilient. They believe they can handle other challenges in life now *because* of their moving experiences.

You know what else these kids feel? Proud. Your child will feel proud as she rebuilds her life by putting herself out there, introducing herself, and jumping into new situations. The early days of hiding in the bathroom stall during lunchtime will soon morph into landing a spot on the basketball or debate team and then sitting with the team at lunch. Her social skills will improve as she learns to navigate an unfamiliar environment. Your child internalizes each victory—whether it's figuring out the school lockers or making the honor roll. She did it and that's incredible.

So, before you worry any further about your kids, take a look at the next two charts that describe what your child's life will be like before and after the move.

Yes, there are going to be bumps along the way, but that's what makes this move a good thing. Your child will be a better person because of it. I know some of you want a number,

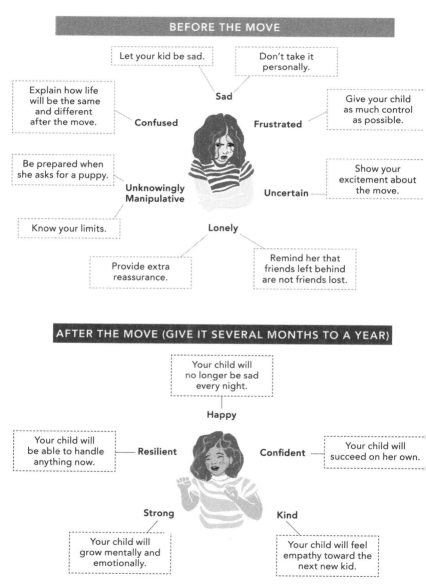

BEFORE THE MOVE

Let your kid be sad.

Don't take it personally.

Explain how life will be the same and different after the move.

Sad

Confused

Frustrated

Give your child as much control as possible.

Be prepared when she asks for a puppy.

Unknowingly Manipulative

Uncertain

Show your excitement about the move.

Know your limits.

Lonely

Provide extra reassurance.

Remind her that friends left behind are not friends lost.

AFTER THE MOVE (GIVE IT SEVERAL MONTHS TO A YEAR)

Your child will no longer be sad every night.

Happy

Your child will be able to handle anything now.

Resilient

Confident

Your child will succeed on her own.

Strong

Kind

Your child will grow mentally and emotionally.

Your child will feel empathy toward the next new kid.

though. How long is this building resilience thing going to take and just how hard will it be for you? In the beginning, I'm not going to lie, it's tough. There will be tears (yours and your kids'). It gets easier, though, and within three to six months, you'll start to get into a routine. By the end of the year, you'll feel settled, and you'll look back on the whole experience and say, "Yeah, we did that." High fives all around.

7

"JUST TELL ME WHAT TO DO!"

Even Han and Chewie go through a checklist . . . and
they're traveling into hyperspace!

— JON STEWART, *The Daily Show with Jon Stewart*

Moving was easier fifteen years ago. I'd put on my rattiest jeans, an old T-shirt, and a comfortable pair of sneakers. Dan and I would drag our stuff into a ten-foot U-Haul truck, lock the back, and slide into our bucket seats as we headed cross-country. Just us and the open road.

Then, Instagram happened.

You might think that adding three kids into our lives complicated the process, but no. It was Instagram. One more item to add to your moving checklist: "Leave out the hairbrush and cute outfit." Okay, fine, you probably have more pressing issues on your mind. However, my goal in this chapter is to help you simplify your decision-making to the point where all you have to worry about is choosing the right filter for that artfully staged shot of your packing tape (#happymoving).

When I met with a mom who was moving from Chicago to Boston she told me she felt exhausted from making all the tiny decisions that go with moving. "I just want someone to tell me what to *do*," she said.

Challenge accepted.

Even if you've moved before, you might find yourself struggling. This is not uncommon. Moving is like having a baby: your memories of the pain somehow get erased so that you wind up doing it again. To help refresh those memories or set the stage for any newcomers, I have provided a week-by-week Moving Checklist in the appendix. It's there for you whenever you need it. The rest of this chapter is a collection of thoughts that go with and beyond the checklist—small thoughts that can make a big difference and wind up saving you time (and money) in the process.

Decluttering is the first step, but you already know that

By this point, you've decluttered by category and not by room, which helps you get rid of more stuff, and makes packing and unpacking easier. Check. ✔

Buy a folder to keep yourself organized and scan important documents

To keep the moving paperwork under control, put it in one folder and remember to keep it handy on moving day. What types of documents do you need in your moving folder? Moving contracts, moving receipts, medical records, prescription information, birth certificates, and school records. Scan all important documents and email them to yourself or save them on your phone. You may not have computer access right away, but you may need these documents for a job interview or for your kid's school. Make copies of your new house keys and set them aside with your important papers. Also, save all moving-related receipts because you may be able to deduct moving expenses on your tax return.[*]

Pack as far in advance as you can

Murphy's Law was made for moving. Basically, anything that can go wrong, will. Whether it's your landlord, your job, or a sick kid, obstacles will come up that make it difficult to pack at the last minute. *Even if you think you've allocated enough time for packing, add 50 percent to that time.* It always takes longer than you anticipate. When we made our second move of ten, I grossly underestimated how long it would take to pack. That ended in tears for me and beloved items were tossed into the trash (RIP, favorite beach chairs).

The first thing to do is collect boxes from family and friends or find free moving boxes and packing materials online. Check websites like Craigslist and Nextdoor or Facebook groups and be sure to pick up free moving materials

[*] Talk to a tax professional about this. You may be able to deduct the cost of packing and shipping your items as well as moving-related travel expenses (not including meals). To qualify, you need to move within a year of starting your new job and you must pass a time and distance test. For the time test, you need to work full-time at your new job for at least thirty-nine weeks in the first year. For the distance test, your new job must be fifty miles farther from your old home than your old job was.

right away because they go fast. Also, ask around at your office or at local stores to see if they plan to discard any boxes and if you can have them. Create several boxes at once to get yourself motivated. For heavy items like books, use small boxes. When the box is half full, lift it. See if it is getting too heavy for you to carry. If so, take out a couple heavy items and replace them with light objects like pillows and puffy jackets.

Label everything. The more detailed, the better. Write down the destination room, the entirety of the box's contents, and add a heart if it contains any favorite items. For example, label a bathroom box filled with assorted items: "Master Bath: bathrobe, slippers, tissue holder, soap dispenser, vanilla candle, hand towels." (Bathrobe + candle = heart label for me.) If you're feeling creative, color-code your boxes with different stickers for each room.

Find a mover or book your DIY truck early

You have a better chance to save money if you plan ahead. If you're using movers, get three binding in-house estimates. This means that the mover will come into your home and take an inventory of your furniture and belongings. The mover will provide you with a binding estimate or a "guaranteed rate" based on those items. It's important to receive a copy of these listed items, often called a table of measurements, so that you and the mover are in agreement as to what will be moved. If possible, schedule these moving estimates close together and try to negotiate prices with the moving company you like most. For DIY trucks, call around for pricing. You may be able to save money by driving twenty minutes farther away to pick up your truck.

How do you find a mover in the first place? You can use the "Find a Mover" search engine on websites like Move.org, Moving.com, or MoveforHunger.org. Type in your current and new zip code, the size of your move by number of bedrooms, and your moving date. Then, companies will call you to set up the in-house estimates. If you use one of the thousand moving companies affiliated with Move for Hunger, the movers will take your nonperishable food items to your local food pantry at no cost to you. So, you're not getting charged to move heavy canned goods and you help your community at the same time.

Along with moving your furniture and belongings, you'll want to think about moving your car. Do you plan on driving your car or do you need to find another way to get it to your new city? If you need to rent a trailer for your truck or want a company to transport your car for you, start checking prices now. Oh, yeah, and don't use a car cover if you decide to haul it yourself.

Set up appointments

I talked to a journalist who lamented her move from New York City to Vancouver. Sure, the city was great, but would she ever find a hairstylist like Val in Vancouver? To this woman, Val was one of a kind, so I reassured the journalist that she would find a strong backup stylist even if she wouldn't be able to replace her relationship with Val.

The lesson here: get everything done *before* you move. Take care of your medical needs first. Get medical records and prescription information from your doctor, dentist, and veterinarian. Transfer prescriptions to your new pharmacy if they aren't linked already. Then, make appointments for everything else—hair, nails, waxing, massages, pet grooming, and so on. Whatever your guilty pleasure is, indulge in it one last time. It may be a while before you experience the same level of (perceived) quality in your new city.

Make flight and hotel reservations early

Reduce stress and potentially save money by making your travel reservations early. This is especially important if you are traveling with pets. Call the hotels and airlines directly, because online information may be wrong.

Some airlines require documentation for your pet *up to two months in advance*, so start to collect the appropriate records as soon as you know you're moving. If your move will require hotel or rental arrangements, choose a place that has a flexible cancellation policy since your plans may change due to unforeseen circumstances. See: Murphy's Law.

Got water? Is it hot?

There are few situations worse than getting to your new home and realizing you forgot:

- To bring your keys
- To turn on utilities
- To schedule internet/cable service

So that you don't make the first mistake, add your new keys to your key ring right now if you have them. You don't want to be one of those people who packed her house keys in a moving box. Not that you wouldn't be in esteemed company. For the utilities, you want to call three weeks in advance to confirm the shut-off and activation dates. Set an alert on your phone as a reminder. Businesses may be closed or have limited hours on weekends, which can lead to an uncomfortable few days without heat or water if you don't plan ahead. *This is a simple task to check off your list, but it can be a major pain if you forget to do it.*

Change of address notification

I included a Change of Address Notification Checklist in the appendix because I don't want to scare you. *Everyone* wants to know about your move, including the bank, the government, and the Department of Motor Vehicles. Register your change of address with the U.S. Post Office to get your mail forwarded, and as a bonus, you'll receive over $750 worth of coupons if you do so online at USPS.gov. (This book just paid for itself.) You can update your address as early as three months prior to your move.

Arrange a school visit for your child

The scariest part for the kids is the unknown. So, call the new school to see if your child can visit before she starts classes. Then you two can find the bathroom ahead of time, walk the route between classes, and ask how lunch works. If you can't make a school visit, that's totally fine. Check out the school's website and look for photos of your child's teacher. Ask the school to pair you with a local family that can answer questions and give advice.

Moving week: Time for those last-minute items

By Moving Week, you're set with doctor's appointments and movers and important documents. You returned your library books and picked up your dry cleaning. You set up your bills for autopay so they don't get lost in the mail. (And remember, there's a week-by-week Moving Checklist to guide you through this stage in the appendix.) Now you only need to survive this one last week to make it to your final, fabulous destination.

Last-Minute Items

1. Finish packing those boxes (you're *so* close).
2. Fill a suitcase with travel essentials.
3. Create a Moving Day Survival Kit (see the appendix) for you, your family, and pets.
4. Pack a Need Immediately Box.
5. Dismantle furniture, if needed.

This week, *your hard work will be rewarded in spades.* The more you decluttered and packed along the way, the easier and less stressful this week will be. Now it's time to pack for the trip, whether it's an overnight bag or a suitcase to last until you and your belongings make it to your new place.

You can find tips for the Moving Day Survival Kit and the Need Immediately Box in the appendix, and there's more information on the big day in chapter 10. As for the Need Immediately Box, I pack that on the last day because it contains items in daily use—like the coffee maker.

Finally, dismantle any furniture that you don't plan on taking "as is." This may be a child's crib, a bedframe, or an elaborate bookcase. Please remember to take pictures before you dismantle anything. Put all the screws in a plastic bag and attach the bag to the underside of the furniture with plastic wrap—avoid tape, which leaves a sticky residue. Label each part. For example, "Right bottom: This side faces out." What seems obvious now probably won't seem straightforward when you attempt to reassemble it. Use bungee cords or plastic wrap to hold furniture pieces together.

That's it. It's not so bad, really. All it takes is some planning and checklists to get you through. If you are moving with pets, check out the next chapter for a few more to-dos to ensure a happy pet moving experience. Otherwise, skip to chapter 9, where we'll start planning that going-away party (and those Instagram shots).

8

———

HAPPY MOVING WITH YOUR PET

"It is hard to be brave," said Piglet, sniffling slightly, "when you're only a Very Small Animal."

—A. A. MILNE, *Winnie-the-Pooh*

My parents bred Himalayan cats when I was a kid. My dad also had a penchant for waiting until my cat-loving mom was out of town to bring home a new puppy for me and my brother. Every cat, dog, and the occasional peacock that ended up at our house had its own personality. Pets, like people, will approach the move in their own way. Regardless of your pet's temperament, there are ways you can help make moving easier for him.

First, think about how your pet handles car drives. Does little Caesar wag his tail and stick his head out the window, envisioning the birds he'll chase at the local park? Or is your pet like my cat, Thomasina, who would cower in her carrier, clawing and trembling in anticipation of another vet visit? If you normally take your pet to places that your pet considers tortuous, she may not pounce into the car ready for a road trip. But you can help her get there.

MAKE YOUR PET CARRIER A HAPPY PLACE

Create a positive association with whatever mode of transportation you plan to use for your dog, cat, hamster, or bird during the move. This might be a pet carrier or your whole car. Try to start this process at least a few weeks before your move. For a cat, put the carrier in your living room with her well-loved toy in it. Let her explore it at her leisure. When she makes up her mind to check it out, reward her with a treat, praise, or extra attention (if she's the kind of cat who likes attention). If she works better alone, give her the space she needs. For a dog, use the carrier to take him somewhere fun that he likes to go. This could be a favorite spot where you walk together or a wide-open space where you can play catch.

GET UP TO DATE ON YOUR PET'S VACCINATIONS

If you plan to travel with your pet by air, the airline will ask for your pet's health certificates. Some airlines require documentation thirty days in advance, so it's important to plan early. Even if you're traveling by car, make sure your pet's care is up to date and your records are complete. This will simplify your transition to a new veterinarian. At your appointment, ask your vet for the following items:

- Vet records
- Vaccination certificates
- Recommendation for a veterinarian in your new city

- Medication for travel, if appropriate
- Refill of prescription medicine
- Transfer of prescription to a new pharmacy

PLAN A SPA DAY FOR YOUR PET

One complaint I often hear from humans is that they can never replace their hairstylist after they move. Imagine how your pet must feel. Why not let your feline feel fancy and fabulous one last time before she leaves home? And your dog doesn't want to be grimy when he's trying to make a good impression with the ladies, right? Clean and manicured pets make for more pleasant traveling companions, so everyone wins here. Whether you do the grooming yourself or spring for a cleaning, your furry friend will feel the love.

CONFIRM HOTEL AND AIRLINE RESERVATIONS OVER THE PHONE

If you're driving, look for pet-friendly hotels along the route. Sites like BringFido.com can help you search through pet-friendly options. In order to ensure that online information is correct, call the hotel to confirm that pets are allowed. When you book your air travel, ask whether your pet will fly with you in the cabin or in the cargo hold. There's limited space in the cabin, so the earlier you reserve, the better your chances are of getting what you want. Airlines may require different types of documentation, so confirm this information over the phone as well.

PACK A MOVING DAY SURVIVAL KIT FOR YOUR PET

Just as you'll have your own essentials packed for moving day, your pet will need some items packed, too. Be sure to include:

- Food, snacks, treats, and bottled water
- Food bowl (disposable if you prefer)
- A secure, well-ventilated crate
- An airline-approved carrier
- Favorite toys
- Litter box or absorbent travel pet pads, paper towels, and wipes
- ID tags with your new address, leash, and collar
- Vet records and medications

HOW WILL YOUR PET HANDLE THE STRESS OF MOVING DAY?

You know your pet best. Will she feel most comfortable tucked away in her carrier in your bathroom or would it be better to ask a friend to take her for the day? Moving day is hectic with many demands on your attention and many precariously propped-open doors. Make sure to keep your pet safe and secure during loading and unloading. If you decide to board your pet, schedule to pick her up *after* the truck is packed and when you're ready to leave your home. Since loading may take longer than you expect, ask the boarding facility if they are flexible with the pickup time and give yourself at least a two-hour buffer.

AN ANIMAL RELOCATION COMPANY CAN BE HELPFUL

It can be tricky to move with pets, especially if you're traveling internationally. Some countries require animals to be quarantined for up to six months (!) prior to entry. Pet relocation companies can help you navigate these issues.

Safety Tips When Moving with Pets

- To minimize the risk of losing your pet on moving day, keep him in a safe, enclosed space (such as a pet carrier). He should be wearing an identification collar featuring your new address.
- Don't place your pet in the back of a moving van or pickup truck. Since furniture can shift and temperatures are unregulated, this is not a safe place for your pet.

MOVING WITH PETS MATCHING GAME

Travel with all important pet documents.

Never transport your pet in the storage area of a truck.

Update collar with new address and current phone number.

Keep your pet in a safe carrier during moving day.

WHAT TO DO ONCE YOU GET TO YOUR NEW PLACE

Ask your pet to fill out a dream home wish list. If she's uncooperative, help her out. Check your new home and outdoor area for potential pet hazards and remove them before you let your pet out of the carrier. Then, it's time to create your pet's sanctuary. Lay out a comfy bed and a soft blanket, maybe a favorite toy, and give your pet the tour. Visit the rooms of your new home together. Show her where to find the food, the kitty litter, the water bowl. Take your dog out for a walk to see the neighborhood, which is also a great way to meet the human neighbors.

STICK TO YOUR ROUTINE

Your pet may be confused by his new environment. Provide a sense of security by keeping up with your routines, whether it's going for a walk at the same time every day or maintaining a food schedule. If you and Wrigley went to the neighborhood dog park every Sunday, continue the tradition as part of exploring your new area.

Use the time after the truck is unloaded for extra snuggles, petting your kitty, or rubbing your puppy's belly. It'll be your post-move meditation and is good therapy for the both of you. Now that your pet is set, it's time to create a moving bucket list. Maybe your pet has a few ideas of her own.

9

YOUR MOVING BUCKET LIST

Goodbye, Old Home, and Hello, Road Trip!

That's why I love road trips, dude. It's like doing something without actually doing anything.
    —JOHN GREEN, *An Abundance of Katherines*

Who says moving can't be a pleasure? Before moving day, enjoy your favorite places one more time or visit new spots you've dreamed of going to for years. Invite friends for a game night to show off your Taboo-playing skills, go for a bike ride along the river, or splurge on an all-you-can-eat chocolate buffet. (This buffet actually exists at the Peninsula Chicago hotel and it's glorious.) They say to live each day as if it were your last. Well, your last day *is* coming, so let's make the best of the time you have left and have some fun.

Let's go back to the Gratitude Journal you made in chapter 1 for some bucket list inspiration for things to do before you leave. Here's a sample of one of my lists.

ALI'S CHICAGO MOVING BUCKET LIST

PLACES TO GO	PEOPLE TO SHARE IT WITH
Lincoln Park Zoo	Family
Children's Museum at Navy Pier	Family
Museum of Science and Industry	Family
Zanies Comedy Club	Friends
Chicago Botanic Garden	Family
Lakefront	Family

EVENTS	
Outdoor movie at local park	Family
Chicago Air and Water Show	Family
Brunch or dinner at our house	Friends

RESTAURANTS	
Local Indian restaurant	Family
Portillo's	Family
Deep dish pizza place	Family
Local ice cream shop	Family
Tapas restaurant	Friends
French restaurant	Dan

What are *you* going to miss after you move? Write it down here or write out your own version on a blank piece of paper.

MOVING BUCKET LIST

PLACES TO GO	PEOPLE TO SHARE IT WITH

EVENTS

RESTAURANTS

If you'd prefer not to write everything down, print out a Google map of your current hometown that shows local restaurants and attractions and start circling.

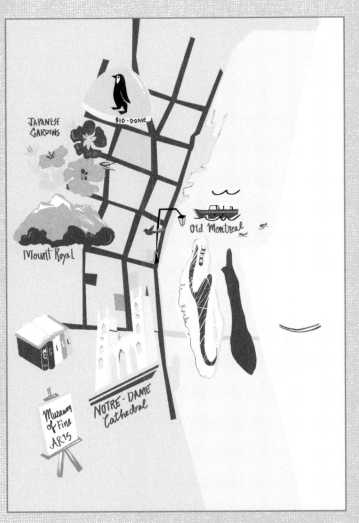

Kids also like to map out activities, so let them circle places worthy of a final visit as well.

SAYING GOODBYE

One of the best parts about moving is getting the chance to tell people how much they mean to you. This kind of opportunity doesn't happen often, so take advantage of the moment and spread the love. Tell your favorite barista that you'll miss her delicious Frappuccinos and infectious smile. Tell the grocery cashier how much you've loved hearing about her pecan pie recipes. Let the everyday people in your life know how much they've impacted you in a positive way.

When it comes to close family and friends, they will want to say goodbye even if they're upset about your decision to leave. Show them you care and make time for proper farewells. You can host a barbecue or meet for coffee. Read on for some other farewell ideas.

Moving party ideas for the multitasker

GARAGE SALE BREAKFAST

Why not combine your garage sale with a get-together? Invite friends to stop by thirty minutes before the garage sale start time for a garage sale preparty. Make it clear that you don't expect anyone to purchase anything, but you want a chance to say goodbye to the neighborhood. Remember to pick up some coffee and donuts for your friends. Garage sales start early.

PACKING OR DECLUTTERING PARTY

Sure, the friends you'd ask to come over to help you pack probably need to be your *really* close friends, but offering chocolate and a bottle of wine can go a long way to show you appreciate their time and effort. Set a goal for yourself, like packing five boxes or purging your books. Then, give yourself the rest of the night off to hang out.

Moving party ideas for the pleasure seeker

BUCKET LIST CHECKOFF WITH FAMILY OR FRIENDS

What's on that bucket list of yours? A spa outing with friends or a day of watching football with your buddies may be the perfect way to relax after a day of packing. Go through your bucket list and invite your crew to join in as you visit your favorite places. Mark each event on your calendar. Envision your upcoming night at the comedy club to stay motivated as you declutter your office junk drawer.

POTLUCK DINNER

As much as you want to have your friends over one last time, you may not want to prepare an entire meal. Instead, invite everyone over for a potluck. For party favors, leave out any items you can't use such as half-finished laundry detergent or unused paint. One woman's trash is another woman's freshly painted guest bedroom.

Moving party ideas for families

PICNIC GATHERING

If you'd rather not host your kids' friends among your moving boxes, then take it outside. Invite families to join you at a local park for a bring-your-own-picnic lunch. Remember to take lots of pictures, so you can make a photo album for your child later.

EMPTY HOUSE SLEEPOVER

You may decide to stay in your house while the movers take your belongings to your next destination. If you plan to move internationally, you may be living in an empty house for a while. Don't waste this opportunity. Invite your kids' friends over for an unforgettable "empty house" sleepover. The kids can play games like Murder in the Dark. All they need is a killer, a detective, and unknowing victims roaming your empty home. Your kids' friends will never forget it. They might have nightmares but, oh, the stories they'll tell later. There's no shortage of fun games that you can play when the house is empty and you don't have to worry about the kids destroying the furniture.

DREAM PARTY FOR YOUR KID

If your child always dreamed of having a birthday party with an unlimited ice cream bar or an overnight campout in your backyard, this is the perfect time to make that dream come true. Sure, we're playing into parental guilt here, but the party will give your child a chance to say goodbye to friends *and* it can make you feel better. (Please refer back to chapter 6: your kid is building resilience and you're doing a great job.)

Parting gifts for friends

Your friends don't expect a gift when you're moving, but they'll appreciate a keepsake. The easiest mementos are pictures—

take tons of them. In addition to texting the pictures to your friends, print out a few to give to them, too. If crafts appeal to you, go out for a painting night where you and your friends take home matching coffee mugs. If your friend has coveted your martini glasses since your first holiday party and you plan to toss them, pass the glasses along. Everybody wins.

Your child may want to give something to her friends, too. She might set aside a toy or a book to give to a friend. Before my son's friend, José Ignacio, moved to Chile, he gave my son his Nerf gun. It's now Joseph's treasured possession for many reasons. Alternately, the kids can make friendship bracelets or create a scrapbook together. If you host a going-away party, leave out a guest book and ask everyone to sign it (kids and parents). This gives friends the chance to say their goodbyes in writing or in pictures, and it's a beautiful way to remember the people in your life after you move.

ROAD TRIP TIME!

Ready for some good old-fashioned road trip planning? I'm here to guide you through an adventure during the actual journey of your move—whether across town or across state lines. This is supposed to be fun, so if the idea of planning anything else stresses you out, ignore me and skip this part of the chapter.

I'm not talking anything crazy cost-wise or time-wise (unless you're up for that). You can visit tons of places around the country that are free or almost free. On the Art of Happy Moving Pinterest page, you'll find ideas for cross-country road trips and unusual tourist destinations. Who wouldn't want to see a gigantic picnic basket in Newark, Ohio, or the Mystery Hole in Ansted, West Virginia? Even a thirty-minute stopover during a multiday trip can rejuvenate you and make for some memorable moments. If you have more time and your budget allows, splurge on a nice hotel and enjoy cities along the way. Alternatively, you can hurry to your final destination and stay in a downtown hotel where you can act like a tourist for the weekend.

Get cozy on the road

Your moving truck or car will be your home for the next few days (or weeks?), so let's cozy it up a bit. Items to bring:

- Your pillow
- A light blanket (perfect for the car or an impromptu picnic)
- Your favorite playlist (you may need a few)
- An audiobook you love (ooh, pick me, pick me)
- Previously downloaded podcasts (don't rely on Wi-Fi availability)
- A cooler with drinks and snacks
- An emergency kit that includes a flashlight (or an LED candle for that glow factor)

Getting around the U.S.A.

Your trip plan will depend largely on the length of the drive and the timing of your move. First, figure out how far you need to go and how much time you have to get there. Let's say you're driving 2,500 miles from Ohio to California. Do you need to make the trip in three days or ten? From there, you can decide on your excursions based on the amount of time they'll take. If you have five extra days, you may be able to squeeze in a visit to the Great Salt Lake in Utah *and* the casinos in Vegas.

If you plan to fly, take a mini-vacay closer to your new home. Making a local move? You can still splurge on a day or night out once you settle in.

Some considerations for the road trip planner

Accommodations: Make arrangements as soon as possible to get the best rates, but find places with flexible cancellation policies. If you're driving a truck with a trailer, ask if there's truck parking on the premises that is safe and well lit (and bring a good padlock). Find out if pets are allowed. While you're on the phone, you might as well ask whether breakfast is included.

Sights: Make a list of your top five destinations and rate them with a fun scale, as shown in the example below.

▲▲▲▲ I cannot miss this. I'm SO excited!!!
▲▲▲   Oh, the stories I could tell if I visited here.
▲▲   This looks cool. Hopefully, I can make it work.
▲   If I'm in the neighborhood, it might be worth a look-see.

Take a look at the sample list I made for destinations between Ohio and California:

Road Trip Wish List

▲▲▲▲   1. Mount Rushmore in Keystone, South Dakota

▲▲▲▲   2. Lake Tahoe, California

▲   3. Lewis and Clark Interpretive Center in Sioux
            City, Iowa

▲▲   4. Jolly Green Giant statue in Blue Earth,
            Minnesota

▲▲▲   5. Devil's Gulch Park in Garretson, South Dakota

Figure out a couple of possible stops on your route and then read up on some history. You'll have time to kill in the car, so ask your copilot to tell you the story behind the places you visit by reading from a guidebook or Googling towns as you pass through. If you're traveling solo, listen to an audiobook about the transcontinental railroad or a podcast about the Wild West. It will make the road trip more interesting. For example, Devil's Gulch Park may not mean anything to you until you discover it's the place where the outlaw Jesse James jumped across a ravine with his horse in order to evade capture. Then, if you decide to try the jump on your own (please don't), a thirty-minute stop becomes a fun photo op to show your friends.

Restaurants: When Dan and I road trip, our diet inevitably consists of fast food. But some preplanning can help you find healthier—or at least more interesting—options. Dan and I once made a thirty-minute detour to find the top-rated donut shop in Atlanta. It closed at 1 P.M. We arrived at 1:01 P.M. as the owner was locking the door. He saw our desperation and let us in, selling us an entire box of the largest, softest glazed donuts for only five dollars. I can still taste them.

To optimize your road trip meals, it can be helpful to plan your approximate driving route and times. Then, prioritize a few special places along the way. Ideally, you'll make it to the restaurant when it's open for business. Instead of eating another drive-through meal, do a quick Google or Yelp search to help you find the local hot spots. Those are the meals you'll remember.

Mmm . . . donuts.

Whether you plan to move locally, out of state, or internationally, find a way to celebrate the occasion. Savor a last tour of your current home, enjoy the journey to your final destination, and then spend some time playing the tourist when you arrive at your new place. If you're currently packing, return to this chapter whenever you need a breather. It'll remind you about the fun activities you want to do before you move. And now, it's time for moving day. You ready? In the next chapter, I have some tips on how to make this the happiest moving day ever. (Chocolate not included.)

10

MOVING DAY SURVIVAL TIPS

When you're moving, your whole world is boxes. That's all you think about. "Boxes, where are there boxes?" You just wander down the street going in and out of stores, "Are there boxes here? Have you seen any boxes?" It's all you think about. You can't even talk to people, you can't concentrate. "Will you shut up? I'm looking for boxes!"
—JERRY SEINFELD, *Sein Language*

Seventy-five percent of us move on our own. But even if you're using movers, you might still pack your belongings or find yourself disassembling furniture. So, it's worth a quick review of how to prep, pack, and move your things even if you're working with professionals.

The Essentials

- Food, water, and snacks
- Disposable dishware and cups
- Box cutters, scissors, and Band-Aids
- Sharpies, Ziploc bags, packing tape, and rubber bands
- Furniture dolly

- Furniture pads or covers
- Bungee cords and plastic wrap
- Ratchet tie-down straps or nylon rope
- Toilet paper
- Garbage bags
- Vacuum or Swiffer and a dustpan
- Hand soap and paper towels
- A sense of humor

First things first, pour yourself a big cup of coffee and put on some comfortable clothes. You may notice that the professionals wear jumpsuits, which don't need to be held up by belts that can damage furniture. The lesson? Try to wear clothes that won't catch on your beloved desk.

HOW TO LOAD A TRUCK

To optimize your truck-loading experience, use:

- a truck with a loading ramp
- a furniture dolly

The furniture dolly will also be helpful when you unload your truck, so ask the truck rental company if you can return the dolly with the truck, or you can buy a dolly to keep for future use.

The first rule of loading is to distribute weight evenly so that the truck doesn't flip over when you're on the road. Place heavy items on the floor of the truck to keep the center of gravity low, making the truck more stable and less likely to tip. A high center of gravity, on the other hand, can cause a truck to roll over on a tight curve like a highway exit ramp. I've seen it happen. It's not pretty. (And no, thankfully, it wasn't my truck.) Weight that's unbalanced from left to right can also cause tipping.

Start loading the heaviest items, like a refrigerator or washer/dryer, into the back of the truck (this is the part of the truck closest to the driver's cab). If you are moving a refrigerator or freezer, remember to defrost it at least twenty-four hours before your move. Now it's time to start loading the other large pieces. Create a border around the edge of the truck with mattresses, bookcases, and flat furniture. Sofas should be placed on end (vertically) to maximize your space in the truck. To lighten your load, remove drawers from dressers and armoires as you load the truck. Once the dresser is on the truck, insert the drawers and use plastic wrap or bungee cords to keep the drawers in place. Then, turn the furniture to face the wall to minimize the chance that the drawers will open. For extra protection, put a mattress between the furniture and the wall. Remember to use a mattress cover because trucks get really dirty.

After the large pieces are in, start building some snowmen: heavy, large boxes at the bottom and smaller, lighter boxes on top. You can also place small boxes on empty bookshelves or in empty cupboards to maximize space. Use ratchet tie-down straps or nylon rope to keep everything in place and strap sections down throughout the loading process. Sofa cushions and pillows in garbage bags or odd-shaped items (such as strollers or hula hoops) can fill in the gaps.

A Few Safety Tips

- If possible, don't leave your moving truck open and unattended.
- Have someone bring items to the truck while the other person organizes the contents.
- Buy a padlock.

PACK THE ESSENTIALS IN YOUR CAR

If you plan to drive your car to your new home, take the most critical and valuable items, like your computer and jewelry, with you in the car. Pack a suitcase with basic clothing and other items you'd want for a weekend getaway or for however long your trip will be. I also recommend packing a Need Immediately box full of items you'll ... need immediately in your new home. These might include:

- A lamp (or battery-powered lantern), light bulbs, flashlights
- Plastic or disposable dishware and a picnic blanket
- Toilet paper (you'll thank me later)
- Garbage bags
- Towels and soap
- Air mattress, pillows, sleeping bags, blankets
- Coffee maker, coffee filters, coffee, sugar packets
- Cell phones, chargers, and electronic devices

If you can fit it in your car, bring a lamp with you because your new place may not have any overhead lighting. A picnic blanket or large towel can create the perfect ambiance for that makeshift dining room. When we moved with the kids to Tennessee, we laid out our blue-and-black picnic blanket, used a moving box as a table, and ate pizza straight from the box. My husband remembers eating fried chicken as kid, perched on top of rolls of carpet during his family's first meal in a new house. These are the Happy Moving moments you'll remember.

WORKING WITH PROFESSIONAL MOVERS

If you want to know the best way to work with professional movers, it's easy. Be kind. Before we take a behind-the-scenes look at what it's like to be a mover, let's assume that everything will be splendid on moving day. Forget every negative moving story that you've heard or that has happened to you in the past. Let it go. Next, let's recognize that our stuff is just . . . stuff.

It's helpful to look at moving day from your movers' point of view if you want to make a happy move. On a typical day, the movers will show up at a shipper's (that's us) house in the morning. They pack and load everything as carefully as possible so that they don't need to deal with a damage claim. Then, the movers drive across the country to your new home and unpack the contents of the truck.

The movers may pick up another load along the way. Imagine another moving day (or two) just like yours crammed in between the loading and unloading of your belongings. It sounds exhausting, doesn't it? The movers work twelve to fourteen hours a day, often not eating until the work is done, and then they travel around the country to wherever the dispatcher sends them next.

So, now it's your moving day. When the movers arrive, they ring your doorbell in the morning, probably having finished another moving job yesterday. They also might have driven through a snowstorm in Philly or dealt with a blow-out tire in rush hour traffic. How should you answer the door? Time for a little quiz.

HOW TO WORK WITH PROFESSIONAL
MOVERS FOR A HAPPY MOVING DAY
A TRUE OR FALSE QUIZ

Answer T for true or F for false after reading each statement.

1. _____ When you get the initial estimate, don't show the movers everything they need to move or pack.

2. _____ When the movers arrive, greet them with "You're late!"

3. _____ Greet the movers with a smile and say, "Hi. Welcome to our home."

4. _____ Introduce yourself and your family to the movers.

5. _____ Offer the movers a cup of coffee or some water as you talk logistics.

6. _____ Don't bother to learn the movers' names. It's only one day, after all.

7. _____ Designate a bathroom in your home that the movers can use.

8. _____ If you are ordering food, ask the movers if they would like some, too.

9. _____ Yell and threaten to sue when something goes wrong.

10. _____ Tip the movers if you are happy with their service.

How'd you do?* It sounds pretty simple, doesn't it? Introduce yourself, remember people's names, and offer a cup of coffee when you've already made yourself a pot. This isn't rocket science. It's simple, common courtesy. You and the movers will be hanging out for the next day or two, and moving day will be much more pleasant if you're all on friendly terms.

There are a few other details you want to consider when using professional movers. Understand your contract and what's included. Will the movers be packing, loading, and unloading? Will you save money if you disassemble/reassemble furniture on your own? Will they be packing everything or only certain items? Remember to keep the table of measurements, which details the items to be moved. You should have received this list when you signed the movers' contract.

Think about the parking situation as well. If you live in a neighborhood where it's difficult to maneuver a large moving truck, will you be charged a shuttle fee to move the items from a smaller truck to a larger one? If you need to block off parking spots for the truck, who takes care of the signage—you or the moving company? Does the move include a stop at a storage facility? Are there parking issues there?

There are other ways you can help make moving day a happy one. Stay out of the movers' way when they're carrying heavy pieces of furniture. Ask if there's anything you can do, and if they say no, believe them. Your elaborately labeled boxes will help the movers determine where to place

* Answers: 1. False. 2. False. 3. True. 4. True. 5. True. 6. False. 7. True. 8. True. 9. False. 10. True.

everything—they don't need you watching their every move like a hawk. If a mover does make a mistake (drops your guitar or scratches your new oak floors), imagine that your best friend did it instead of flipping out. Accidents happen when heavy objects are moved. Act professionally with the expectation the moving company will do its best to make the situation right.

Whether you make the move on your own or have some help moving day will come and go, and before you know it, your furniture has arrived. You have arrived. You're only a few cardio and strength workouts away from being moved in, which sounds like the perfect justification for pizza and chocolate to me. Don't worry about getting everything unpacked right away. You have time.

Now it's on to the fun stuff.

11

———

WHAT MAKES YOUR
HOME HAPPY?

So what if my house wasn't perfect?
It was perfect just the way it was.
—JOANNA GAINES, *The Magnolia Story*

Creating your new, happy home is the best part of moving. There aren't any rules. You're not staging a house to sell anymore. No more Zillow photos, no more Realtor advice, no more need to target immaculate, magazine-cover perfection. Forget about what you think *other* people would like. This time, it's about you and what makes *you* happy. It doesn't matter if you own or rent, whether you live in a studio apartment or a four-bedroom house, or whether you have a budget of $50 or $50,000. You can design a home that makes you smile every time you walk through the door.

Wow, you say, *that's quite a promise*. It is—and designing a happy home doesn't just happen from dumping your box marked "Dining Room" onto the dining room table. There is a method to creating a joyful place.

The process is a lot like trying a new cake recipe—there will be some comforting ingredients you already have (like your beloved couch) and others you'll discover out in the world, whether in the form of a stunning design blog or a new favorite restaurant. In this chapter, I'll show you how to find what you love and how to create a fresh, blissful space using the items that moved with you as the foundation.

USE YOUR NEW FLOOR PLAN TO HELP YOU VISUALIZE THE SPACE

Even if you're reading this chapter months before moving day, you can begin to design your dream space now. The first thing you'll need is a floor plan of your new space. This will help you determine where furniture will go and it will help you imagine future happy moments. You might picture yourself curled up by the fireplace, reading a murder mystery during a thunderstorm, or seated on your balcony with a steaming cup of coffee, watching the pedestrian traffic below. You can imagine all kinds of scenarios by looking at a simple layout on a sheet of paper. To get a floor plan, ask your landlord or the current owner. Many apartment complexes provide floor plans online. If for some reason you aren't able to get a copy of the floor plan, go through the pictures and videos you took during that weekend scouting visit.

GATHER THE ITEMS YOU LOVE

Once you move into your new home, first sort through a few boxes that you drew a heart on during the packing phase. That way, you can surround yourself with framed photos, well-loved books, and cherished coffee mugs before you unpack your bathroom cleaning supplies. These little heart notes are like a gift to yourself, and they make for a nice, cheerful boost when you need it most. If you unpack items that you realize no longer bring you joy, now is a great time to discard them. To help with your design budget, make a deal with yourself. For any item you sell, you can keep that money in a separate account and use it to buy new furniture and accessories.

FIND YOUR INSPIRATION

After reacquainting yourself with your possessions, it's time to gather inspiration. This is a moment to dream. In the age of Pinterest, there's no excuse not to. With hundreds of images to look at and collect, it's easy to create a free, portable mood board for your home (or for each room if you prefer). If you're new to Pinterest or feel overwhelmed by the sheer amount of content available, you can check out the Art of Happy Moving boards on Pinterest, where you can find happy home ideas. If Pinterest isn't your thing, rip out pages from home design magazines and keep them in a folder. Go to your local library and check out a stack of design books. Take pictures of rooms you love so you have easy access to them on your phone.

Inspiration can come from anywhere. It might come from a luxury hotel, the feel of sand between your toes, or the sight of a waterfall after a hike. What is it about the ambiance in certain places that really speaks to you? Get pictures, take notes, and see if you can identify some specific features that make you feel the way you do in those places.

WHAT MAKES YOU HAPPY AT HOME?

Nice décor and good flow between rooms don't make a home *happy*. We don't live inside of a catalog. So, what is it about your home that makes it special? Is it the cozy spot where you do the crossword on Sunday mornings? Is it your vegetable garden? Maybe it's your master bedroom, where you can decompress after a long day. To me, my home is happy when I can smell chocolate chip cookies baking. Even though the kitchen is a mess, eating cookies with my kids is the best. My point is this: It's not really about how the house *looks*. It's about how the house *lives*.

YOUR IDEAL HOME

Circle as many answers as you'd like. There may be more than one response that applies to you.

1. **When you get out of bed in the morning, you like to:**

   a. Feel the soft carpet under your feet
   b. Look out the window to catch a glimpse of the day
   c. Hear the birds chirping outside
   d. Smell the lavender oil on your nightstand

2. **As you walk into the bathroom, you feel happy because of the:**

   a. Warm rug on a cold morning
   b. Beautiful towels hanging straight on the rack

   c. Sound of the shower turning on

   d. Smell of the vanilla soap

3. **Standing in your kitchen, you love to:**

   a. Feel the clean countertops and polished floors

   b. Look out the kitchen window to see the garden

   c. Listen to bacon sizzling

   d. Smell the coffee brewing

4. **Your favorite part about the family room is:**

   a. The comfy sofa and chenille blankets

   b. The well-designed layout and the artwork

   c. The sound of the football game on TV

   d. The scent of fresh-cut lilies on the table

5. **As you sit down at the dining room table, you're most excited about:**

   a. The comfortable and sturdy chairs

   b. The artfully displayed place settings

   c. The in-room sound system

   d. The meal you're about to eat

6. **Your home office is perfect for you because:**

   a. It's ergonomically designed

   b. It looks just like a photo from a magazine

   c. It's quiet and out of the way

   d. There's a plate of cookies next to your computer

7. You like playing in the kids' room because:

    a. It's filled with fun textures
    b. The toys are nicely organized
    c. The giggles never stop
    d. There's a gumball machine on the desk

8. In your dream outdoor space, you can:

    a. Sit comfortably and enjoy a beverage
    b. Take Pinterest-worthy photos
    c. Hear the sounds of birds chirping
    d. Smell the herb garden

9. If you could spend an entire day at home alone, you would:

    a. Find the coziest spot in the house, get snuggled in, and read a book
    b. Find the most beautiful view and enjoy your favorite hobby
    c. Pump up the music and dance like no one is watching
    d. Cook up something delicious as a treat for yourself

10. Your ideal atmosphere for entertaining friends:

    a. Has a casual and relaxed vibe
    b. Would make Martha Stewart proud
    c. Involves a guitar
    d. Includes cooking on the grill

It's okay if you picked multiple answers for each question. You just want to get the wheels turning about what makes your home happy. Did you notice a pattern in your responses? Tally them up, with one point for each question.

If you picked mostly As, you are a Feeler. You are sensitive to the way items feel. You're the type of person who takes off your winter gloves when you walk into a clothing store because you can't shop without touching the fabrics. *Tips for you:* Find textures that feel good against your skin. Decorate with soft throw blankets and luxurious linens. Plush bath mats, a couch you can sink into, and comfortable dining room chairs will help you create your happy home.

If you picked mostly Bs, you are a Looker. You are a visual person who admires how objects appear. You see beauty in colors. You might find a clean palette soothing or maybe you prefer loud, saturated hues. If something is pleasing to the eye, it makes you smile. *Tips for you:* Visual clues from magazines or design blogs will be especially helpful when you're decorating. Focus on removing clutter and keeping your home organized. When designing, consider the pops of color that make you happiest and sprinkle them throughout your home.

If you picked mostly Cs, you are a Listener. You are in tune with the sounds in your environment. When you close your eyes in a room, you feel at peace as you take it all in. Maybe being surrounded by music inspires you, or the sounds of nature calm you. *Tips for you:* Pay special attention to designing your auditory environment. Change the doorbell to a soothing melody. Choose an alarm clock with pleasing audio effects, like crashing waves or nature sounds. Consider purchasing a wireless speaker so you can listen to music throughout your home.

If you picked mostly Ds, you are a Sniffer. You can literally smell and taste happiness. As you enter an Italian restaurant, you breathe in the scent of the sauces and garlic bread, and you can't help but smile. Your happy home is one filled with delicious aromas and flavors. *Tips for you:* To create your happy home, you don't need to be a baker or a chef, though you might enjoy that. If you don't cook, buy prepared meals that you can slide into the oven and let the aromas waft throughout the house. Buy luxurious soaps and lotions. Use scented candles, oils, or aromatic plants. Keep a small herb garden by your kitchen window or splurge on fresh flowers.

Now that you know what senses are most important to you and you've identified specific items that you love, you're ready to design your dream happy home. In the next chapter, we'll go room by room to help you achieve that goal.

12

CREATING A HAPPY HOME WITH SPECIAL NOOKS AND PLACES TO ENTERTAIN FRIENDS

There's no place like home.

—L. FRANK BAUM, *The Wonderful Wizard of Oz*

Whenever Dan and I move, we choose to find ways to make our home happy and unique. When we lived in student housing in California, we painted our walls blue, yellow, and orange. In our rental house in Chicago, we bought a colorful rug for the kids' bedroom, so they'd have a soft spot to play on the wooden floor. It didn't matter that we would be living in each place temporarily. It was still our home, and we wanted to make it special.

To create a happy home, you need three things: your favorite colors, your favorite objects, and your favorite people (whether you live with them or not). In this chapter, we'll spend time thinking about each of these, and I'll show you how to blend them into custom homemaking specifically suited to your personality, tastes, and needs. Some of these tips are geared toward people moving into a multiroom dwelling, but the general spirit of this chapter can apply to any type of housing. After all, at the end of the day, a home isn't really tied to any one space. It's a feeling you bring with you wherever you go.

CHOOSING COLORS FOR YOUR HOME

I'm not an interior designer, but I do know what I like, and I gravitate toward blues, reds, and yellows. I understand that we'll need to neutralize our home if and when we sell it, but for now, my home office has turquoise walls. And I love my office. I adore those walls. They make me immeasurably happy.

What colors inspire you? What makes you smile? If you're not sure, check your closet to see what colors you typically choose for your wardrobe or use the chart on the next page to help you.

It's worth noting that your favorite colors might not necessarily be what you want for your design aesthetic. Maybe you love orange, but you prefer neutral tones like beige, ivory, or gray for your home. Don't worry—you don't need to paint your walls orange if that's too intense for you. Instead, use neutrals when you paint and sprinkle a bold color throughout your living room or kitchen with accessories like vases, blankets, or picture frames.

A word on painting your walls: As we discussed in the home-staging chapter, paint will transform your home. The paint hue that delights you will make your space feel distinctive. Ideally, you would paint before you move in, but we've been in that enviable position only once, so I know it's not always possible. Even if you live in a 375-square-foot apartment

	EFFECTS THE COLOR HAS	BEST ROOMS TO USE THE COLOR
Red	Stimulates, dramatizes, empowers	Dining room
Orange	Excites, cheers, evokes enthusiasm	Exercise room, good accent color
Yellow	Energizes, brightens, uplifts	Kitchen, dining room, bathroom, entryway
Green	Calms, balances, refreshes	Kitchen, living room
Blue	Cools, comforts, creates serenity	Bedroom, bathroom, dining room
Purple	Relaxes, spiritualizes, encourages creativity	Bedroom, dining room
Black	Strengthens, stabilizes, demonstrates power	Best used in small doses as an accent
Brown	Invites, secures, conveys warmth	Office
White	Purifies, cleans, unifies	Bathroom, living room
Pink	Warms, soothes, softens	Bedroom

like we did in California, you can get around a full room by pushing your furniture into the center of the space and covering it with a tarp or painter's cloth.

Let's go room by room to design your space, and please feel free to skip rooms that don't apply. If you want to make quick changes, simply refer to the senses chart for each room. This will give you an idea of what items to include based on the senses that are most important to your environment. If you want to do more, think about what colors you want for each space and who will be sharing the rooms with you (as a guest or a permanent resident). There's also a room-by-room chart in the appendix that you can use as a checklist.

CHILD'S BEDROOM

If you have kids, I recommend you set up their rooms first. When we moved to our rental house in Chicago, I rushed to unpack the kids' rooms while Dan picked up the kids from his parents' house in Ohio. I arranged the bedding, set up their bookshelf, and displayed my son's favorite truck and my daughters' cherished dolls. I added their new winter coats and boots to the closet as a special surprise. Since my son and eldest daughter shared a room at the time, I divided the room and placed their personal artwork over each bed. When Victoria, Joseph, and Charlotte arrived, they cheered when they saw the unpacked room, their treasured toys, and their pristine winter gear.

FEELER	LOOKER	LISTENER	SNIFFER
Flippable sequined pillow	Organized closet	Stereo system or iPod	Potted plant
Beanbag chair	Floating shelves for display	Gentle alarm clock	Clothes laundered in favorite detergent
Soft carpet	Trunk to store toys	Ceiling fan	Gumball machine
Desktop globe	Labeled storage bins	Ambient noise maker	Gym shoes stored elsewhere
Microfiber flip chair	Cork board for photos	Open windows to hear distant train whistling	Emptied trash can

When you set up your child's room, it helps her feel calm and secure when she first arrives. Of course, as she gets more comfortable in her new home, you can give her a chance to be creative and show her personality in the space as well.

Favorite color(s). Please note here:

_____

Once your child picks his favorite color(s), consider painting the room that color. Alternately, if you prefer less of a commitment, buy a lamp, pillow, or bulletin board in the color she loves.

Favorite objects

Does your child love his collection of Matchbox cars or football trophies? If so, display them. Create a space where he can draw comics or learn about constellations under a makeshift tent. Budget so that he can have one new, exciting feature in his room. Then, take him shopping and have him test out beanbag chairs or a cool art table. When your son feels involved in the decision-making, he'll feel more in control and more excited about the move.

Favorite people

Who does your child plan to hang out with in his room—friends, Mom or Dad, siblings? Create spaces to encourage story time with a parent, gaming with buddies, or late-night conversations with his brother. Also, as much as our kids love us, *privacy is important*, especially as kids get older. So, give your child a space to do homework or read a book without interruption.

KITCHEN

My family spends more time in the kitchen than anywhere else in our home. With three meals a day and the inevitable dessert creation by my daughter, we're in the kitchen ALL the time—prepping, cooking, and cleaning. This is why unpacking the kitchen is a top priority for us when we move somewhere new. We want this room to feel like home right away.

FEELER	LOOKER	LISTENER	SNIFFER
Smooth kitchen surface	Clear sink space	Sizzling bacon	Basil or rosemary garden
Soft kitchen towels	Chic light fixtures	Motivating music	Bowl of strawberries or melons
Plush kitchen mats	Organized cutlery	Popcorn popping	Lemon kitchen cleaner
Ceramic storage containers	Similarly colored and sized dishware	Kettle boiling	Pumpkin spices
Clean floors	Closed storage	Coffee brewing	Slow-cooker meals

Favorite color(s). Please note here:

_____

What time of day do you use the kitchen? If you use it mostly as a space to drink your morning coffee, consider a color that energizes you. If you typically use the kitchen at night, you may prefer a more soothing tone.

Favorite objects

Before you unpack, spend a few minutes to make a game plan for your kitchen gear. Items often stay in the same drawers for years, so a little planning will go a long way. Plan for easy access to the items you use often. For example, place your cutlery in an accessible drawer that's close to your dishwasher or sink, and store your pots and pans by the oven. For a happiness boost, showcase your favorite items. Put your Hawaii coffee mug on an open shelf, prop open that braised short rib recipe, and add a hook for your "Boss of the Kitchen" apron.

Favorite people (yourself included)

Your ideal kitchen may be the place where you can enjoy your tea and a crossword puzzle in peace. Or maybe your kitchen will be the spot for Thursday night happy hours or Sunday family get-togethers. Depending on your entertainment needs and desires, consider barstools for a kitchen island, a breakfast nook with a banquette, or a chair by a kitchen window.

MASTER BEDROOM

No room is more personal than your bedroom, so make it *you*. In order for you to have a sanctuary amid the moving chaos, prioritize this room. Unpack your bedroom boxes, even before you set up the living room.

FEELER	LOOKER	LISTENER	SNIFFER
Luxurious linens	Decluttered nightstand	Ambient noise maker	Freshly laundered linens
Down-filled pillows	Dramatic focal point	In-room music setup	Vanilla candle
Comfortable mattress	Symmetrical lighting	Soothing alarm clock	Vase of roses
Plush chair	Armoire for clothing or TV storage	Ceiling fan	Dryer sheets in drawers
Soft rug or carpet	Repetition of similar art frames	Carpet or rug for sound reduction	Cedar chips or hangers in closet

Favorite color(s). Please note here:

_____

Be creative with color here. This is your space. It does not need to flow with the rest of the house.

Favorite objects

Unless a moving box is labeled "Master Bedroom," try to keep it out of your bedroom. Your bedroom should be your oasis: a place to unwind, relax, and be intimate. This is a good time to go through one last round of purging as well. Before you hang up your shirts and put away your shoes, make sure that everything you own is an item you love. Your closet should make you happy, not stress you out.

Favorite people (yourself included)

Imagine you have twenty minutes to yourself at night. How would you spend your time? Create a tray with some favorite items. Maybe you'd choose a book, a glass of wine, the TV remote control, or a bowl of popcorn. Place this tray, your "happy tray," on your nightstand or at the foot of your bed. Then, make it a habit to create a happy tray every night, filled with a few objects that bring you joy before you go to sleep.

BATHROOM

You should clean every room of your house before you store or display your possessions, and this is especially true in your bathroom—you probably won't be emptying the contents under your sink for a weekly dusting. So, give the bathroom a good scrub down while it's still empty.

FEELER	LOOKER	LISTENER	SNIFFER
Soft bath towels	Big framed mirror	Open window	Baby powder
Rich bath mat	Symmetrical sconces	Shower radio	Lavender soap
Comfortable toilet paper	Clear counter space	Waterfall faucet	Scented lotion
Luxurious bathrobe	Drawer dividers	Leak-free fixtures to avoid dripping	Emptied trash can
Heated towel rack	Stylish towels	Bath mats to dampen sound	Fan to prevent mold and mildew

Favorite color(s). Please note here:

_____

Whether you want a sleek, modern style or a romantic, charming ambiance the color you choose for your walls will have a big impact in this smaller space.

Favorite objects

I love the saying "Let the store be your storage." Buying in bulk may save you a little money, but think of it this way: Would you spend three extra dollars every month to have a clutter-free bathroom? If your answer is yes, skip cheaper bulk products that can crowd your bathroom cabinet and instead enjoy your clean, decluttered space. Also, if you didn't throw out your old makeup or half-empty hotel shampoo bottles before the move, now's your chance.

Favorite people (yourself included)

You deserve a bathroom haven. Put up the fancy towels. Organize the space so that only one soap, lotion, and shampoo bottle is on display. Light a candle, set out a bath bomb, and lay out slippers to create your personal spa.

LIVING ROOM

We'll learn more about creating good habits in the next chapter, but you can start to think about whether you want

FEELER	LOOKER	LISTENER	SNIFFER
Comfy couch or reading chair	Bold artwork	Crackling fire	Burning fire
Plush rug	Natural daylight with sheer curtains	Piano or guitar	Scented candle
Faux fur or chenille throw blankets	Appropriate furniture spacing dimensions*	Sound system	Vacuumed carpet
Mixture of textures: silk pillow on leather couch	Closed media cabinet	Silence	Fresh floral arrangement
Smooth polished woods	Organic elements	Open windows to hear thunderstorm	Potted plant

*If you have the space, allow fourteen to eighteen inches between your couch and coffee table. End tables should be about the same height as the arm of a couch or chair. There should be a minimum of two and a half feet of space between furniture pieces to allow for a comfortable walkway. The largest piece (most likely your couch) should face your focal point.

to make any life changes after you move. If so, your living room can make an excellent location cue to help spur those new routines. If you plan to read more, fill a bookshelf with library books or your reading wish list. If you want to spend more time with family, place board games or puzzles within easy reach. Set up a place for your yoga mat if you want to exercise every day. Do you want to focus on personal relationships? Display photos of family and friends. Not only will they remind you of your goals, but being surrounded by loved ones and happy memories will also feel good.

Favorite color(s). Please note here:

_____

Your living room or family room is the space where you'll unwind, relax, and entertain. You may find that neutrals or pastels help to create the relaxing scheme you desire. On the other hand, this is the place where you'll spend most of your time, so if you prefer more invigorating hues, don't be afraid to use color and personalize your space.

Favorite objects

What items energize you? Whether it's trinkets from your global travels or a well-loved journal, the living room is the perfect place for these inspirational items. A less motivating item, your television, will probably reside in your living room as well, and you'll want to decide how prominent it will be in the space (and in your life). If you want to downplay the presence of the television, you can arrange furniture so that the focal point is a window or the fireplace instead of the TV. You can also find artwork or a media cabinet to hide the TV when it's not in use.

Favorite people (yourself included)

The living room is the most versatile room in your home. You might use it as a place to work, play, entertain, or seek refuge—all in the same day. Depending on how you want to use the space, you can create seating arrangements to accommodate game nights or to encourage intimate conversation.

DINING ROOM

It's increasingly rare these days to have a dedicated dining room. You probably don't entertain in your dining room every day, and may even use it for other purposes, such as a communal work space. If this is the case, you'll want to pay particular attention to the lighting. Carefully designed lighting can transform an everyday workplace into a more romantic setting by night.

FEELER	LOOKER	LISTENER	SNIFFER
Comfortable dining chairs	Crystal or contemporary chandelier	Mood-setting music	Cheese tray with fresh fruit
Contrasting textures: metal, wood, and stone	Lighting on dimmer switch	Fizzy drink poured over ice	Dish of chocolate-covered caramels
Soft fabrics on seating	Pinterest-worthy table arrangement	Sizzling fajitas	Baked bread
Luxurious tablecloth	Unique centerpiece	Clinking of glasses	Bouquet of flowers
Smooth rug	Splashes of vibrant color	Windows open to outside to hear wind rustling	Open bottle of wine

Favorite color(s). Please note here:

_____

Even if you're steering clear of loud colors in other parts of your home, the dining room is the perfect place to use a bold color. This is where you'll celebrate momentous occasions and milestones—if there were ever a room that called for indigo or fuchsia, this would be the one.

Favorite objects

The problem with the dining table is that it's a flat surface begging you to leave purses and unsorted stacks of mail on it. Resist the siren call. Find a spot that is *not* your dining table—another place where your computer bag can rest after the workday, a hook where a backpack can hang. Check mail by the recycling bin so you can toss junk mail immediately.

Favorite people (yourself included)

How will you use this space? Even if you don't plan to entertain often, try to keep the clutter to a minimum so you have a place to relax when needed and so you can invite friends over when you want to. Also, it doesn't hurt to have a small tray easily accessible for throwing together a plate of cookies and a cup of coffee on short notice.

OFFICE

The turquoise office walls that I love so much are also the turquoise walls of our guest bedroom. All I need to do is pick up my laptop and scattered papers, and the space transforms into a place for a guest to put on her makeup. Whether or not you have a dedicated work space, you can create a comfortable office area that is conducive to productivity.

FEELER	LOOKER	LISTENER	SNIFFER
Comfortable chair	Decluttered desk	Desktop waterfall	Aromatic potted plant
Squeezable stress reliever	Memo board or wall calendar for organization	Ambient noise maker	Scented oil diffuser
Ergonomic computer setup	Striking accessories	Favorite playlist	Natural cleaning products
Contemporary glass	Task lighting	Conch shell to hear sound of sea	Candy dish
Polished woods	Displayed book collection	Purring cat	Clean filters in HVAC system

Favorite color(s). Please note here:

_____

Present company excluded, many people prefer calming colors such as browns or neutrals to inspire efficient working. Warm hues can help create a soothing and professional work environment.

Favorite objects

With portable devices and Wi-Fi, it's possible to create an office nook anywhere in your house. Just look for a space that inspires you, whether because of the view or the lack of clutter. Using a desk lamp or swing-arm lamp will help make the space more personal and functional.

Favorite people (yourself included)

Unless you entertain clients at home, your office space will probably include only you. However, you may decide that you like to work amid the mix of the household activities. If so, find a place in the living room or kitchen where you can set up shop. Substitute the sofa table or an end table with your desk and set up your workspace by the couch. If you prefer a quiet place, find a spot where you can close the door to prevent interruptions.

OUTDOOR SPACE

Although the kitchen is where my family and I spend most of our time, it's our outdoor space that I love most. When we lived in Ohio, Dan and I had a small balcony with two rocking chairs and numerous potted plants, and we would hang out there and talk after work. These days, our kids play in their tree house while Dan tends to his vegetable garden, and I read on the porch listening to my little waterfall. Wherever we've lived, we've made our outdoor space a place where we can relax.

FEELER	LOOKER	LISTENER	SNIFFER
Hammock with soft pillows	Twinkling string lights	Gravel path that crunches underfoot	Herb garden
Padded bench in shady spot	Brightly colored outdoor pillows	Outdoor waterfall	Outdoor grill
Sun-drenched spot with zero-gravity chair	Hurricane lamps	Bird feeder	Fresh mulch and dirt
Stone steps	Manicured lawn	Wind chimes	Freshly cut grass
Outdoor patio rug	Orderly garden	Fire pit	Aromatic flowers and plants

Favorite color(s). Please note here:

_____

Even the smallest outdoor space has oasis potential. Don't worry about decorating rules. Be eclectic if that suits you. Encourage daydreaming and a sense of adventure. Choose bold colors.

Favorite objects

Take risks in your outdoor space. Do you love sundials or fairy gardens or vintage baskets? Anything goes outside. Have fun with it.

Favorite people (yourself included)

Your outdoor space is the perfect place for entertaining. There's no need to worry about formalities or making a mess. Invite neighbors over for a potluck or for drinks. Create a special place for yourself for times when you're craving some downtime. Even in small spaces, you can add string lights, flowers, and a folding chair for the perfect spot to enjoy your pumpkin latte on a fall morning.

It's the taste of a home-cooked meal, the laughter of friends, and the freshly laundered sheets that make your house feel like home. Focus on these small details to help you feel more at home in your new space. It's easy to create a happy home— just fill it with the items and people who make you happy. To discover how to be happy *outside* of your home after your move, read on.

13

BREAKING OLD HABITS AND FORMING NEW GOOD ONES

It's a bit drastic, though: moving to another house, city, or country just so you can walk to work rather than drive.... The vast majority of us don't have the desire or, indeed, the resources to relocate just to shake up old habits.
—JEREMY DEAN, *Making Habits, Breaking Habits*

Humorist David Sedaris read somewhere that to quit smoking, he should shake up his routine. So, he moved. To Tokyo. After smoking a pack and a half a day, Sedaris went cold turkey on the flight to Japan. His plan? To use his new surroundings to help him forget his suffering. "More than my products [the patches and lozenges]," Sedaris says, "I think it helps that everything is so new and different: our electronic toilet, for instance."

On his flight back home, Sedaris calculated how much it cost him to quit smoking.

COST OF QUITTING

Round-trip airfare to Tokyo

Three-month apartment rental

School tuition to learn Japanese

+ Unused patches and lozenges

$20,000

It took only $20,000 and a few months of suffering, but Sedaris did it.* The old habit was broken.

MOVING IS YOUR CHANCE

Moving disrupts your daily routine and creates the *perfect* time to make a change. You've been given a gift. Evidently, your gift is valued at approximately $20,000. When researchers studied successful habit changers, 36 percent of their subjects credited *moving* for the change.† That's more than one in three people who made a successful life change *because*

---

* Sedaris describes how he quit smoking in his book *When You Are Engulfed in Flames* (New York: Little, Brown and Company, 2008).

† "36% of successful habit changes were associated with a move to a new place." Gretchen Rubin, *Better Than Before: Mastering the Habits of Our Everyday Lives* (New York: Crown Publishers, 2015), p. 119.

they relocated. It would be a shame not to take advantage of this opportunity for a fresh start. Moving—even just across the hall—takes care of the toughest part. It breaks the daily feedback loop (at least temporarily) and creates an opportunity for you to alter your habits.

CHOOSE YOUR GOAL—BIG OR SMALL

You may want to focus on one change at a time. For example, after we moved back to Chicago, Dan and I decided to switch to decaf coffee in an effort to decrease our caffeine intake. (It goes against my profession to drink coffee without caffeine, so let's keep this little secret between us.) It was hard at first, but our initial cravings quickly gave way to a new addiction: feeling healthier. Before long, we had also stopped drinking caffeinated soda and started to eat healthier and exercise more. After a lifetime of chugging Diet Coke, I no longer craved it. We didn't set out to change any major habits, but one minor change snowballed. *It turns out that using self-control in one aspect of your life can create a domino effect, positively impacting other areas of your life as well.*

Moving doesn't come around every day, though, so you may want to aim higher than switching to decaf. If a whole life makeover is more your style, I've included a Moving Resolutions chart in the appendix that can help you track your lifestyle changes.

WHY YOUR MOVE WILL HELP YOU SUCCEED

Here's the lowdown on your brain: It's lazy. Or, put another way, it's efficient. Over 40 percent of the time, your brain is on cruise control. It knows how to brush teeth, put on clothes, drive to work, fire up the computer, make dinner, and go to bed. Your brain conserves energy for more important tasks, like remembering to call the utility company before you move or reading this book.

How does your brain juggle all this input? Among other things, it looks for cues, follows a routine, and then pats itself on the cerebellum as a reward for a job well done. You get out of bed in the morning and see your toothbrush (cue), you brush your teeth (routine), your mouth tingles, and you see yourself smile in the mirror (reward). It's not long before you start to crave that clean, fresh smile. That craving is what transforms this routine into a habit. While brushing your teeth is a good habit, the same loop—cues, routines, and rewards fueled by cravings—occurs with bad habits.

THE GOOD NEWS
Because our brain likes habits, it's easy to establish different routines and create new good habits.

THE BAD NEWS
Bad habits never go away. They lurk in the background, so you need to establish new routines to override them.

BAD HABITS DON'T GO AWAY

Habits are like paint jobs: you can't make a bad habit disappear, but you can cover up one you don't want with a new one. Charles Duhigg, the author of *The Power of Habit,* calls this the Golden Rule of Habit Change. The way to change a bad habit is to keep the same cue and the same reward, but you insert a new routine. For example, let's say three o'clock hits and it's time for your daily afternoon chocolate boost. Instead of reaching for a candy bar, go for a short walk outside and get the energy you need from a few minutes of fresh air.

CHANGE FAMILY HABITS

You can also take this opportunity to create new rules for the entire family. Right as we were getting ready to move back to Chicago, Dan and I had reached our parental limit of so-called no-spill sippy cups hidden all around the house. The move presented a golden opportunity.

"Listen up, kids! New family rule: anytime you eat or drink, you have to sit at the table." Oh, the joys of dictatorship. In the short term, we celebrated—no more cups of spoiled milk buried in the couch. Years later, I appreciate how many hours we've spent hanging out at the table together at snack time and how many fewer hours I've spent vacuuming the basement. Even this relatively minor change had a ripple effect on our family trajectory.

CHANGING YOUR HABITS

What are your habits now, and what would you like to change? Do you want to exercise more, change your appearance, spend more time with family and friends, put in more effort at work, improve your sleep, learn a language, take up gardening, read more, eat out less, learn to cook, take up karate, create a minimalist home, or something else? Did anything pop into your mind as you read about David Sedaris's move to Tokyo to quit smoking? What would you do if given the opportunity? Oh, wait. You *have* been given the opportunity. What will you do with it?

After I move, I want to make this one change in my life

_____

_____

I want to do it because

_____

_____

(This motivation—your *why*—will help you achieve your goal. Keep your motivation in mind whenever you feel like you might go off track.)

I believe that I can do this. (Circle one.)

Not a chance   **Absolutely!**

1   2   3   4   5   6   7   8   9   10

Am I breaking a bad habit, forming a good habit, or both? (Circle one.)

Breaking a bad habit

Forming a good habit

Both

Whether you are breaking a bad habit or forming a good one, you need to figure out the cue, routine, and reward for that habit. Write out the answers to the following questions to help you achieve your goals.

BREAKING A BAD HABIT

What's the habit?

_____

When do I do it?

_____

Where do I do it?

_____

Who else is around?

_____

How do I feel when I do it?

_____

What's my cue? (Circle all that apply.)

Time of Day   **Place**   **Certain Person(s)**

Visual Cue   **Specific Emotion**

Answer the following questions as many times as needed to address all the cues you circled.

Cue:

_____

Can I take the cue away in my new environment? (Circle one.)

Yes   **No**

If "No," why not?

_____

What's my routine or ritual? In other words, what does my body do when it goes into autopilot mode?

Routine:

_____
_____

What's my reward?

Another way to think of your reward is to imagine what you are *really* getting out of the habit you are trying to break. Observe your own behavior for the next few weeks to understand why you binge-watch TV or eat cookies when your kids aren't looking. (I would *never* do that, kids.) If you eat the cookie, is it because of boredom, hunger, a need for an energy boost, or an excuse to take a break? Once you know your reward, what you *truly* get out of the habit, you can create an alternative habit with that same reward.

Reward:

_____

What else can provide me with the same reward?

Some examples of reward substitutes are eating a different snack to curb hunger, going for a walk to get an energy boost, reading a magazine to take a break, or calling a friend for social interaction.

_____

_____

Can I change my daily routine to incorporate my alternative reward? (Circle one.)

Yes   No

How will I change my routine?

_____

_____

_____

FORMING A GOOD HABIT

The great news is that your brain *wants* to form habits. So, in the case of forming good ones, it's actually on your side. What positive changes do you want to make in your life? What cues can you use to help you?

What new habit do I want to form?

_____

What's my cue? (Circle all that apply.)

Time of Day

Place

Certain Person(s)

Visual Cue

Specific Emotion

Cue:

_____

Routine:

_____

_____

Reward:

_____

_____

To establish a new routine, a plan of attack can be helpful. If you want to eat healthier, create a weekly meal plan or do some batch cooking. To exercise more, sign up for specific classes at the gym or use physical cues like putting your running shoes by the front door. Let's say you want to learn to be more patient. Use time as your cue and schedule three minutes of meditation after you wake up but before you brush your teeth.

If you decide to use time as your cue, pick a regular event instead of a specific time of day. According to Jeremy Dean, the author of *Making Habits, Breaking Habits,* "Researchers have found that the best cue for a new habit is something that happens every day at a regular time."[*] To maximize your success, don't tell yourself that you will do something daily at seven

---

[*] Jeremy Dean, *Making Habits, Breaking Habits: Why We Do Things, Why We Don't, and How to Make Any Change Stick* (Philadelphia: Del Capo Press, 2013), p. 141.

in the morning or three in the afternoon. Instead, tie it to a current routine and choose to do it after your morning shower or your afternoon snack break.

HOW LONG DOES IT TAKE TO ESTABLISH A NEW ROUTINE?

You're ready to make some positive changes, but you probably want to know how long it's going to take. Well, I have the answer. *Sixty-six days.*[*] Yep, that's what the research shows. I love that it's so specific. Also, it's okay if you mess up every once in a while. Just because you miss a day or two doesn't mean you need to start back at zero. Roughly two months is what it takes to put a new habit in place. You can totally do this.

FINAL TIPS FOR SUCCESS

Take small, manageable steps toward your goal. It's more important to form the habit and establish the routine. Get your shoes on in the morning and go for a five-minute walk every day this week. That's much more effective than running three miles on your first day and then quitting. Find a way to hold yourself accountable. Use an activity tracker or schedule the time for exercising on your calendar. Finally, find someone to help you. Rope your roommate into a daily walk or tap into a local biking group to help you stay motivated.

[*] Dean, *Making Habits, Breaking Habits,* p. 5.

Now that you've laid the foundation for some improved routines, it's time to take a look at your new community. In the next several chapters, we'll cover everything you need to know to make a good first impression, meet some cool people, and create lasting friendships.

14

WHERE CAN YOU MEET NEW FRIENDS?

I had said that I felt I needed to try to find girlfriends, but what I really wanted were down-to-earth chicks who drank Strawberry Hill slushees nonironically, and who would respond to an invitation of "Let's go to a wine tasting and a day spa" with the same sort of horrified reaction as if someone had said, "Let's go join the circus and then burn it to the ground."

—JENNY LAWSON, *Let's Pretend This Never Happened*

Six months. It took me six months to meet someone who would become a close friend in Knoxville. I never anticipated that it would take me that long to find a friend. In retrospect, six months isn't an eternity. But when I lived it, I wondered if I would *ever* meet someone. I know, so dramatic.

It's hard to move somewhere you don't know anyone. Where do you meet people? How do you become friends? It can be overwhelming if you don't know where to start. The truth is that there isn't one standard approach to making friends because we each have different friend needs. Nevertheless, once you know what you want, I can show you where to find it and how to get it. For those of you who can be impatient at times (like, erm, me), I can also show you how to speed up the friend-making process.

First things first: what do you want and need from your friends? Once you determine your friendship goals, you can refine your search. Feel free to circle all responses that apply.

FRIENDSHIP GOALS

HOW MANY LOCAL FRIENDS DO I NEED TO BE HAPPY?

0	4–5
1	6+
2–3	

HOW OFTEN DO I NEED TO SEE MY FRIENDS?

Daily	Biweekly
Weekly	Monthly

I WANT MY FRIEND TO BE SIMILAR TO ME IN THESE AREAS:

Age	Job
Marital status	Education
Kid status	Location
Religious beliefs	Political beliefs

MY PREFERRED WAY TO HANG OUT:

Getting coffee	Getting drinks
Watching a movie	Attending a concert
Volunteering	Playing sports
Gaming	Going for a walk
Other: _____	

MY FAVORITE FRIEND SETTING IS:

One-on-one
Small, close group
Large gatherings

THE IDEAL TIME TO BE WITH MY FRIENDS IS:

Weekdays   Morning
Weekends   Afternoon
                                  Evening

I WANT MY FRIEND TO BE:

Funny	Respectful	Protective	Honest
Good listener	Successful	Playful	Sarcastic
Adventurous	Spiritual	Trustworthy	Confident
Accepting	Smart	Quirky	Athletic
Transparent	Dependable	Beautiful	Encouraging
Kind	Supportive	Nurturing	Impressive

Use these friendship goals to help you figure out what you want, not to limit your options. Also, it's hard to find *one* friend to fulfill *all* of your relationship wants and needs. That's usually too much to expect of someone. If you're looking for a laid-back lunch buddy, ask your coworker to join you at the taco truck on Fridays. To get your adventure fix, meet someone through a rock-climbing group. By creating a few friend circles, you can satisfy your various social needs.

WHERE CAN YOU MEET THESE FABULOUS PEOPLE?

To meet people, you need to show up. Yes, moving is exhausting and will make you want to curl up and binge-watch TV. I get it. And you can do that . . . once in a while. But I recommend putting in the effort to make friends sooner rather than later. The longer you wait to leave your apartment, the harder it will be to take the first step. Friends will not magically appear at your doorstep, so it's up to you to find them. The place to find friends is where you are. Existential? Totally. But it's also the truth.

In order to make friends, we need to be physically close to people. While virtual friendships can provide social benefits, you should look for someone local you can meet for coffee or who will bring you soup when you're not feeling well. In addition to being physically close to your future friend, you also need to see her often and for extended periods of time. So, the ideal person would be someone you see on a daily or weekly basis.

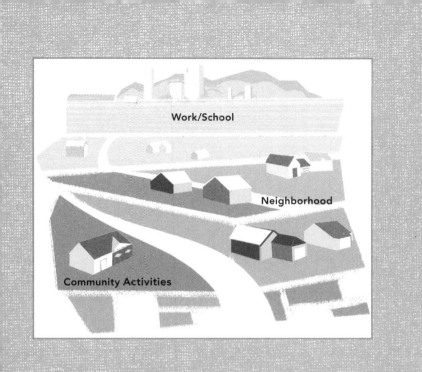

How to make friends at work or school

Work or school is a logical place to start since you see the people there automatically. You can start small by saying good morning to someone every day. You can chat about your weekend or upcoming vacation plans. To get to know someone better, learn about her hobbies or her family and really *listen*. The next time you see her, ask about her weekend trip with the in-laws or about her marathon prep. To build stronger relationships with your coworkers, seek opportunities to spend time with them during the workday and outside the office.

WORK/SCHOOL

Join the work sports league
Volunteer to lead a project or workshop
Invite a coworker to join you for lunch
Travel to work conferences
Attend professional social events
Carpool

How to make friends in your neighborhood

To create friendships in your neighborhood, it's up to you to create the opportunity for interactions. In other words, you need to make the effort.

The more someone sees you and interacts with you, the more likely they are to become your friend. This is known as the Law of Familiarity.* Face time is important. To create a bond, the

* Jack Schafer with Marvin Karlins, *The Like Switch: An Ex-FBI Agent's Guide to Influencing, Attracting, and Winning People Over* (New York: Touchstone, 2015).

Start a book club

Set up a garage sale

Ask for help

Spend time in your yard

Take daily walks

Shop local

Join the homeowners
association

Help your neighbors

NEIGHBORHOOD

people in your neighborhood need to see you. So, get off the couch and out of the house as much as possible. Linger in the yard, take long walks, or sort through your mail while standing in the mail room.

This will sound obvious, but it bears saying: when you make other people feel good, they will like you more. So, help your neighbors. If you're snow blowing your sidewalk, do your neighbor's sidewalk, too. Set up a lending library where neighbors can borrow books from your collection. Also, don't be shy about asking for help or advice. Email the neighborhood group and ask for recommendations for a plumber. Requesting assistance can be endearing, but be careful not to overdo it.

How to make friends in your larger community

There are unlimited opportunities to get involved within your community. The key is to engage in an activity that you love because it will bring you joy, not just because you want to meet people. Your passion and enthusiasm will be evident and authentic, which are attractive qualities. If your sole purpose is to find a friend, however, your desperation will show. (I know, because I've been that person.) You're much more likely to make a true friend when you are being yourself and having fun.

COMMUNITY ACTIVITIES

Volunteer

Sign up for a sports team

Attend a Meetup event

Become active in local politics

Use your skills to teach

Attend a local place of worship

Take an adult education class

Get a gym membership

Think about what you love, what you're good at, and what you want to learn. Then, figure out how you want to spend your time. Are you a phenomenal baker? Offer to teach a class at the local recreation center or provide baked goods for Sunday services. Have you always wanted to learn Italian? Take an evening class. When your activity aligns with your passion, you will find immediate common ground with others. A shared cause or purpose can create a more profound starting point for friendship. And the more you give to the community, the more you will get back.

YOUR FAST-PASS ACCESS TO MAKING FRIENDS

You know what you want and where to get it, but you want to speed up the process. In this section I'll explain how to get on the fast track.

5 Ways to Make Friends Faster

1. Make friends before you move.
2. Look for others who are new in town.
3. Cast a wide net.
4. Welcome people into your home.
5. Be the type of friend you want your new friend to be.

1. Make friends before you move.

This is an easy step, but one most people overlook. We're so busy with the move that we don't think about making friends until we get there, except to occasionally worry that we won't. Save yourself some heartache and start the friend search early. Start by reaching out to your current network. Tell everyone you know where you plan to move. Someone will know *someone* who lives in Sheboygan or San Antonio. Ask to be connected and follow up with that someone.

There are three reasons to make a connection before you move. First, this person can help you through the transition period. He can help you decipher neighborhoods or give you the inside scoop on the best hiking trails. Second, you'll know one friendly face when you arrive and that's priceless. It doesn't matter if this person is older, younger, married, single, female, or male. It will just be nice to know someone. Finally and most important, your acquaintance can introduce you to other people in town. That's the golden ticket. *It's much easier to go from one friend to two friends than from no friends to one.*

2. Look for others who are new in town.

You don't have to move to another country to feel like an outsider. Sometimes we move to places where people have a tight circle of friends they aren't looking to expand. Maybe you've moved to a place where everyone has known one another since kindergarten or where everyone belongs to a church or a country club where you'll never be a member. You are not alone. There are other people in your town who feel like they don't belong, too.

To avoid feeling excluded, look for others in your situation—namely, look for other newcomers. Join new-in-town Meetup groups or come to my book signings to meet others who've recently moved. If you're a new parent, ask local hospitals or religious organizations if they have support groups. Be vocal about your recent move whenever you make small talk. Even if the person you are speaking with grew up in the area, she might know someone who moved into town last month. Ask her to connect you.

3. Cast a wide net.

It's hard to know who you'll click with when you start your friend search. To maximize your chances of finding that good friend quickly, extend invitations to a large group of people. How do you invite a large group when you don't know anyone? Why, by using the bring-a-friend approach, of course.

BRING A FRIEND

Let's say a friend introduces you to Sarah before you move to San Francisco. Sarah moved to the area last summer. After your move, you attend a Meetup bike ride where you meet Caitrin. Even though they don't know each other, you invite Sarah and Caitrin to a free concert. A couple of weeks later, you ask Sarah and Caitrin if they'd like to join you at a DIY art studio and you tell them to invite a friend or two. Sarah brings Kristen and Caitrin brings Jess. You have a great time and decide to plan another event next month. This time Ann, Julia, and Virginia Grace join you as well. Within a few outings, there are now eight of you hanging out together.

SEND OUT A MASS INVITATION

If you prefer not to use the bring-a-friend approach, you can just invite people from different areas of your life to come together. Send out a mass text or email inviting people to join you for an outdoor movie or an art exhibit. Include people you've met at work, in the neighborhood, or through your activities. In order to find fun outing suggestions, sign up for alerts from the local city calendar, the library, or a concert venue.

In my experience, the success rate on these mass invites is about 15 to 20 percent, so have appropriate expectations. People may have prior commitments or they may not be interested in that particular activity. Try not to take it personally and invite them again the next time. If someone says no several times without an explanation, take the hint and focus your friend attention elsewhere.

If casting a wide net feels uncomfortable, remember that people like to be included, even if they don't accept your invitation. Try the mass invite or bring-a-friend approach once or twice to see if it works for you. If not, that's okay, too. Either way, you'll soon want to concentrate on building friendships on a one-on-one basis.

4. Welcome people into your home.

The warmest welcome you can give someone is an invitation into your home. Your home doesn't need to be fancy or decluttered or anything extraordinary—it just needs to be you. When you invite people into your home, they feel more connected to you. They can admire your family photos, get a sense of the music you enjoy, and see what books you like. People can learn more about you in ten minutes at your home than in ten weeks at the office.

If you consider yourself introverted, hosting others at your house can be ideal. You can choose who will be there, how many people will be there, and what kind of activity you'll do together. Themes make entertaining easier with ready-made conversation starters, so hosting around a holiday or an event such as the Super Bowl or Fourth of July can take the pressure off. You can use the wide net approach and invite everyone you know, or make it low-key and invite someone over for coffee.

5. Be the type of friend you want your new friend to be.

Look back at your friendship goals. To make friends and form lasting friendships, you need to be the type of friend you want to attract. Be kind, listen, and bring joy to the lives of others. If you're not searching for someone who is sarcastic or likes to gossip, avoid acting like this yourself.

It's easy to forget the effort you put into building your old friendships, but of course those took time and care to set up as well. Look at it this way—if you did it once, you can do it again, and the effort will be well worth it. I know, I know . . . if you're anything like me, you crave that comfort of close friends and you'd like it again, preferably ASAP. Sadly, it doesn't work that way. It takes time to create friendships. If it's been a while since you've found yourself in this situation, and you'd like to brush up on your small talk skills, read on. Social butterflies, please feel free to skip ahead to chapter 17, where we'll talk about how to make the most of living in your new town.

15

BODY LANGUAGE AND SMALL TALK

Tips for Attracting New Friends

You can make more friends in two months by becoming genuinely interested in other people than you can in two years by trying to get other people interested in you.

—DALE CARNEGIE, *How to Win Friends and Influence People*

When we moved to Knoxville, I wanted to meet my new best friend right away. But after some trial and error, I learned that a few other steps come first. Before you can become friends with a stranger, you need to get to know her. If only I had known this *before* I invited myself to a Knoxville moms' established playgroup. Friendship is a gradual process that starts with a smile or a hello. Some steps may be harder than others, but soon you'll feel more comfortable using your body language to attract friends and you'll be making small talk with everyone.

BODY LANGUAGE CREATES YOUR STORY

You walk into a bookstore and see a good-looking guy wearing jeans and a clean white shirt. He heads toward the café.

with his shoulders back and his chin up. He smiles a small smile. He approaches the counter, looks up at the barista with his arms by his sides, and asks, "Can I please have a medium coffee, cream only?" He looks around the café for a place to sit. The barista calls, "Mike. Medium coffee, cream only." Mike smiles, thanks the barista, and sits down at a nearby table.

That's scenario one. What do you think of Mike? If you stood by Mike at the checkout counter, would you smile at him? Create a story about Mike. What's he like?

Scenario two: You walk into a bookstore and see a good-looking guy wearing jeans and a white shirt with a small stain. He looks down as he walks toward the café with his shoulders hunched and his lips pursed. He approaches the counter, crosses his arms, looks up at the board, and asks, "Can I have a medium coffee, cream only?" He takes out his phone as he waits. The barista calls, "Eric. Medium coffee, cream only." Eric takes his coffee and sits down at a nearby table.

What do you think of Eric? How does he compare to Mike? Why? If we play spot the difference, how many differences can you find in the two scenarios?*

Chances are good that you like Mike more than Eric. Let's break down why that is. They're equally good-looking, so we can take looks out of the equation. First, there's the small stain on Eric's shirt. It's not a huge deal, but we notice it. We're willing to overlook it, but our minds subconsciously note

---

* I spy seven differences that shape our opinion of Eric: unclean shirt, defeated posture, pursed lips, crossed arms, no eye contact, being on his phone, and bad manners.

that he cares less about his outward appearance than Mike does. Next, Eric's posture looks defeated. It's unclear whether he's sad, angry, or tired, but he's not exuding confidence. His closed facial expression doesn't act as an invitation either.

When Eric gets to the counter, he crosses his arms. Now Eric looks defensive. Instead of looking at the barista, he keeps his eyes on the menu. This sends off signals that he does not want to engage in conversation. Eric forgets to say please when he orders and he spends the rest of the time on his phone. Eric's body language screams, "Don't talk to me." That's fine if Eric wants to be left alone. But if you've just moved somewhere new, don't be Eric.

THE SNEAK ATTACK:
5 EASY BODY LANGUAGE TIPS

If you follow a few basic rules of body language, you'll quickly become a friend magnet. I call this technique the SNEAK attack—Smile. Neatness. Eye Contact. Arms Open. Kindness—mostly because I like cool acronyms. But also because it works.

When I talk about body language in my family seminars, the kids learn SEA instead of SNEAK. Why? For starters, neatness isn't as important when you're eight. Plus, kids know to be kind. It's us grown-ups who forget sometimes. A simple "please," "thank you," and "excuse me" can go a long way. But I'm getting ahead of myself.

Use the SNEAK attack to make new friends

Smile
Neatness
Eye Contact
Arms Open
Kindness

S IS FOR SMILE

As teenagers, my friends and I would spend hours in a novelty store called Sparkle Plenty. It sold fuzzy pens, funky alarm clocks, and T-shirts with life-altering advice. One T-shirt read, "Smile. It makes people wonder what you're thinking about." Not one to pass up words of wisdom from a T-shirt, I started to smile for no apparent reason. And it worked like a charm. Sure, I got funny looks on occasion, but for the most part, I would get a smile in return.

That's the thing about smiles. They're magical . . . lucky charms if you will, and the benefits of smiling cannot be disputed.

- Smiling releases feel-good chemicals such as dopamine, endorphins, and serotonin into your brain, which makes you feel happier.
- When you smile, it makes other people happier because it gives them a sense of familiarity and connection.

- Smiles are contagious. Your smile will get you a smile in return.
- A smile shows you are friendly, making it more likely that people will want to be your friend.

Okay, so we all agree that smiles are good for you, your social life, and your aura. Most people are fine with smiling at people they know; it's a whole other thing to smile at people you don't. It's okay if smiling at strangers doesn't come naturally to you—you are putting yourself out there, sending a signal of openness (there's a reason you don't smile at two o'clock in the morning on a subway car), and giving people the chance to reject you by looking away or potentially judge you (*What if they think I look crazy?*). For these moments, a little practice can build your armor:

1. Get in front of a mirror.
2. Smile for the camera.
3. Think of something that makes you laugh (cat videos, text autocorrects, your best friend, whatever you need).
4. Let your smile spread slowly from your mouth to your eyes.
5. Try out different smiles for that gorgeous face in the mirror.

Now that you've practiced at home, take it outside. However, not everyone will or should receive your top-notch smile. Give a small smile to a stranger you pass on the street and bust out the genuine smile for someone you've seen in your apartment complex that you'd like to get to know better.

N IS FOR NEAT

Dan and I do our fair share of home improvement projects, so I've gone out in public covered in paint on more than one occasion. (Always buy that extra gallon of paint. You'll need it.) I've never made any friends during those outings and people keep their distance from me. As unfair as it may seem, people will judge you based on your appearance because it's the only information they have available. So, keep it neat—at least while you're in the making friends stage.

I don't want to cramp your style, but keep in mind that certain aesthetics announce "Back off!" These include uncombed messy hair, sloppy makeup, dirty clothes, and T-shirts with offensive language. It's important to recognize what your appearance says to others, especially if you're sending out vibes you don't intend to. Keeping it simple and clean will help make that good first impression.

E IS FOR EYE CONTACT

Remember Eric? He looked at the menu when he ordered instead of making eye contact with the barista. Eric seemed distracted, disinterested, or maybe even rude. That's not the impression you want to give when you're in the friend market. You want to appear engaged, interested, and friendly. It doesn't matter whether you are ordering coffee or trying to strike up a conversation with someone at work—look the other person in the eye. If eye contact feels uncomfortable to you at first, it's okay to look at the other person's nose or between their eyes. She won't be able to tell the difference.

A IS FOR ARMS OPEN

One way to publicize that you are open to meeting people is to keep your arms by your sides. When you cross your arms, you communicate anger or defensiveness. Even though I'm *always* freezing, I avoid crossing my arms to stay warm because I don't want to give the wrong impression. Your body sends off negative signals when you cross your arms.

To keep your friend options open, literally keep yourself open. Stand with your feet shoulder-width apart, shoulders back, chin up, and arms by your sides. When you sit, maintain the same confident upper-body posture. The funny thing I've learned from people's moving stories is that friendships happen in unexpected places. It doesn't matter whether you are at the bus stop or at the post office—don't cross your arms.

K IS FOR KINDNESS

In his monumental book, *How to Win Friends and Influence People,* Dale Carnegie sums up how to make new friends: "Don't criticize, condemn, or complain." When you're moving, you should consider this instead: "Don't criticize, *compare,* or complain."

When Cindy moved from Los Angeles to Austin she complained about *everything.* She criticized the pace of life in Austin, the hairstylists, and the dining options. Cindy compared every woman she met to the friends she left back at home, thinking none of them matched up in the sophistication department. Cindy says, "It's the worst thing I ever did. I know people thought I was such a witch."*

It didn't take long for Cindy to realize that *she* needed to change if she wanted to be happy in Austin. "I opened my eyes," says Cindy. "I looked around and these women were amazing: well read, well educated. It was my own snobbery that kept me from seeing that at first." Cindy learned not to criticize, compare, or complain. Once she stopped her negative behavior, she started to make friends. She even met her friend soulmate, something Cindy never imagined could happen in her fifties.

Watch out for sabotaging snobbery. If you just moved from Washington, D.C., to Sarasota, Florida, no one wants to hear how much you miss the political action of D.C. If you move from New York to anywhere else, don't complain about the lack of entertainment options or how you could never eat a bagel outside of the City. It doesn't matter if you're right. Yes, your old city may excel in one area that your new city does not. All that your neighbors will hear is criticism of *their* city and their homes.

Boost your confidence with your body language

We've discussed how to use body language to make an impression on others, but it also impacts how you feel about yourself. When you set your shoulders back and hold your head up high, you feel more confident than when you adopt

---

* Quote changed by one letter to keep my PG rating.

a slouched or defeated position. Unfortunately, in today's environment, we spend way too much time hunched over our phones or computers, with slumped shoulders and heads down. Slipping into bad posture habits on a regular basis translates into our feeling less positive and confident about ourselves.

If you want a quick confidence boost before entering a new social situation, strike a power pose. Imagine a superhero with her arms on her waist, her chest puffed out, and her head held high. Assume the power pose whenever you need it, whether it's before you go to work in the morning or in a bathroom stall before you mingle at a party. In Amy Cuddy's book *Presence*, she recommends taking on a confident pose to help you through a challenge.

> By taking up as much space as you comfortably can in the moments preceding the challenge, you're telling yourself that you're powerful—that you've got this—which emancipates you to bring your boldest, most authentic self to the challenge.[*]

To make good posture and positive body language a habit, find a cue that will remind you to readjust your body. When you click "send" on an email, put your shoulders back. After you respond to a text, smile. As you walk through a doorway, hold your head up high. When you see a crack in the sidewalk,

[*] Amy Cuddy, *Presence- Bringing Your Boldest Self to Your Biggest Challenges* (New York: Little, Brown, 2015), p. 243.

take long, confident strides as you walk down the street. Use whatever triggers you need to remind yourself that positive body language will make you feel more confident. Plus, it will attract others to you.

What body language should I use during a conversation?

The SNEAK attack can be deployed anytime, whether you are at a reception or at a crosswalk. But what should you do when you are in a conversation? You should continue your SNEAK attack and add two more moves: *lean in* and *copy the other person's body language.*

   Lean in. All this requires is for you to physically lean your body toward the person who is speaking. If someone is sitting next to you, lean in and do *not* cross your arms (or legs, if you can help it).

   Who seems more interested in the conversation?

Copy the other person's body language. Do what your older sister used to get mad at you for doing: copy her when she talks. But be sure to match only the body language, not everything she says. Some people call this mirroring or mimicking body language, but the terms mean the same thing. Copy away. Try it with loved ones first and ask if they noticed when you mirrored them. Surprisingly, your mom won't know that you put your left hand on your hip after she put her right hand on her hip. She'll just be impressed by how engaged you were in the conversation.

Now that you have the body language down, it's time for the next step: making small talk. I have tips for the introvert in all of us.

HOW TO MAKE SMALL TALK

First of all, don't worry about saying the right thing or sounding witty. Other people are too preoccupied with what they plan to say to notice what you are doing. Remembering this can make small talk less intimidating. Besides, to have a successful conversation, it's much more important to listen and to learn about the other person.

Your small talk game plan

Every time you meet someone at work or in your apartment complex, an opportunity arises to make a connection or maybe even interact with your new best friend to-be. To prepare for these encounters, pick a specific goal for yourself. If you love chatting with strangers, consider setting a target number: How many people can you make small talk with in one day?

What is your small talk goal for today? (Circle one.)

| Say hi to someone | Break the ice | Introduce yourself | Learn something |

Step 1: Say hi to someone. Your open body language and friendly smile may encourage people to say hi to you first. If not, make the effort to say hello yourself. Switch it up with phrases such as "morning," "good afternoon," or "howdy" if you prefer. Do whatever feels good, but be sure to greet everyone you meet and remember to say goodbye. As you check out from Target, say, "Thank you. Have a great day!" Practice talking to strangers at every opportunity.

Step 2: Break the ice. Since you recently moved, you're in an excellent position to break the ice. You can ask for directions or for restaurant recommendations. You can go traditional and ask your neighbor for some sugar. You have the best excuse in the book, so work it. Say, "Hi! I'm new in town. Can you tell me where I can find a good coffee shop?" or "What's your favorite grocery store? I still don't know the area very well."

If the situation doesn't call for a "Hey, I'm new in town" approach, go with one of the old standbys: compliments and the weather. Say, "I love your necklace. Where'd you get it?" or

"This weather is crazy, isn't it? I can't believe it's still snowing in May." The point of an icebreaker is to get a conversation started. It's not a test of how brilliant or funny you are, so keep it simple.

Step 3: Introduce yourself. Take a moment to say, "By the way, I'm Ali." As you say this, put out your hand for that firm handshake (if it feels appropriate). Include some extra information to help the conversation flow after the initial introduction. "By the way, I'm Ali. I just moved from Chicago and I'm loving this warm weather." Depending on the situation, you can talk about what department you work in or what teacher your kid has. The more information you give, the more information you will receive in return.

Step 4: Learn something. You can declare victory when you learn the person's name (and remember it!) or after you've learned a new fact. A good way to discover something is to ask open-ended questions, such as "Do you have any fun plans for the weekend?" or "What did you do over the holidays?" In contrast, a question requiring a yes or no answer is unlikely to give you as much information. If you ask, "Do you like living in this neighborhood?" (a closed question), then follow up with an open-ended question like "That's great. What do you like most about it?"

Step 5: Say goodbye. Like George Costanza, go out on a high note. End the conversation before it dwindles. Regardless of the length of your conversation, end it by saying goodbye to give you closure. If you chatted for a while, say, "It was really nice speaking with you. I hope to see you again soon. Bye!" Leave the possibility open to future conversations. If the conversation went well, extend an invitation to continue it later: "It was fun talking with you, and I'd love to do coffee sometime. Are you free next Sunday by any chance?"

Interesting Conversation 101

To have a good conversation, it's critical to be an active listener. This is great news for introverts. When you're talking with someone, look for clues about what the other person likes to talk about. Then, try to get more information from her about that topic. Set a goal to share one fact about yourself, which could be anything from your recent move to your love of hot air balloons. Take a minute to figure out what clues you want to leave. This allows you to craft the story you want to share with the world.

Topics to Avoid

| Politics | Religion | The Great Pumpkin | Family or health problems | Taxes |

Researchers have found that the *number one way to bore others* is to complain about your problems.[*] It's not a surprising conclusion, but it's a good one to note. Also, avoid emotionally charged subjects that can lead to conflict, or topics

[*] Ann Demarais and Valerie White, *First Impressions: What You Don't Know About How Others See You* (New York: Bantam Books, 2004), p. 126.

that will inevitably end with a complaint—whether that's work, your boyfriend, or how the movers damaged your front door. The purpose of small talk is to keep the conversation light, entertaining, and fun. Wait until you've formed a solid friendship before moving on to heavier topics.

SHOW THEM WHAT YOU'VE GOT

Confidence is attractive. Recognize your strengths and use your body language to signal your confidence. Prepare yourself for conversations by choosing topics that get you excited.

WHAT EXCITES YOU?

Circle three of the topics from the following list that interest you. Then, jot down a few notes for each of your choices.

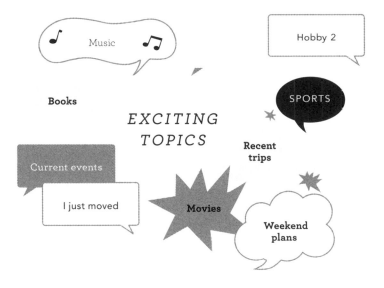

Music

Hobby 2

Books

SPORTS

EXCITING TOPICS

Recent trips

Current events

I just moved

Movies

Weekend plans

Passion and enthusiasm are contagious. If your eyes light up, the listener will love to hear about your rafting trip on the White Salmon River. If you feel insecure about a topic and you know it will come up, you can do one of two things. You can either stop feeling insecure or you can use a diversionary tactic to switch to another topic.

When you start making small talk with strangers, fake your confidence if you have to. The more you put yourself out there, the more self-assurance you will gain. It just takes practice. Use the SNEAK attack whenever and wherever you can. If you focus on listening to others and making them feel good, they will think you are awesome.

16

HELPING YOUR KID MAKE NEW FRIENDS

You can't be that kid standing at the top of the waterslide, overthinking it. You have to go down the chute.

—TINA FEY, *Bossypants*

I host family workshops where I teach kids how to make friends after a move. When the kids first walk into these events, they look down at the ground, uncertain where to sit. I smile and call them over to the front of the room. As I begin to talk, their faces are serious, their eyes attentive. They *want* to learn this stuff. Making friends is important to them.

One of my tips to the kids is: don't cross your arms. There's a shuffle in the back as the adults rush to put their arms by their sides. The kids laugh. By the end of the hour, the kids are all standing up straighter. They smile at one another and introduce themselves. It's fun to watch their confidence grow after learning and practicing some body language strategies.

Before you dive into the tips in this chapter, know that *it's going to be okay.* Your child will make a friend. It may not happen the first day or the first week, but it *will* happen. So, try not to put too much pressure on your child. Instead of asking, "Did you make a new friend today?" you can ask, "Did you meet someone nice today?" Realistic expectations are much more likely to get a positive response.

The following tips can give your child—whether she's a toddler or a teenager—the self-assurance she needs to make it through those first few weeks in a new place.

> **Tips for Helping Your Child Make New Friends**
>
> - Find out what type of friend your child wants.
> - Discuss places where your child might meet that friend.
> - Teach your child the basics of body language: SEA.
> - Practice a few icebreakers together.
> - Be a good role model.

WHAT KIND OF FRIEND DOES YOUR CHILD WANT?

For many kids (who are we kidding—for many people), their greatest anxiety is that they won't be liked. You can help minimize this fear by refocusing your kids' attention on themselves. It's as easy as asking them what kind of friend they want.

Depending on your child's age and temperament, he may say he wants a friend who is nice and you can move on to the next question. If you want to delve deeper, ask your child to look at the Friendship Goals chart in chapter 14. What kinds of qualities does she look for in a friend? This discussion can help your child understand that she has a *choice*, that she can decide who she wants to have as a friend.

When you help your child develop friend goals, he'll learn that he has control over the situation. Instead of worrying "Will anyone like me?" he can take his time to evaluate options and consider "Who would make a good friend?" He can *choose* who his friends are and not feel like he needs to jump into the first group that accepts him. Your child should be kind to everyone, of course, but you should encourage him not to feel desperate to make a friend right away.

Older children identify with groups, and your child may want to identify with a new group after the move. Ask your child to circle any group on the chart below that sounds like a

FRIEND GROUPS

Anime/ comic books	Artists	Athletes	Band	Cheerleaders
Chess club	Choir/ chorus	Computers/ gamers	Drama	Goths
Hip hop group	Hipsters	Mathletes	Musicians	Partiers
Popular kids	Preppies	Religious group	Rockers	ROTC
Science club	Skaters	Smart kids	Student council	Surfers

good fit for her.* It's important to note that these groups aren't mutually exclusive. You can be a popular kid *and* a smart kid *and* a musician *and* a gamer.

Where Can You Meet This Type of Friend?

As we discussed in chapter 14, proximity matters. Your child can meet people in the neighborhood, at school, or through activities. To meet kids in the neighborhood, set up a lemonade stand and play outside in the front yard. Go for bike rides and spend time at the local playground. If it's hard to pry your child away from a screen, use Pokémon Go to explore the neighborhood. For activities, your child may want to continue soccer or chess club, but she might also want to try something different. Ask the school about available extracurricular programs both at school and in the community. Sign up for neighborhood online groups to get the inside scoop and read the flyers posted around town.

TEACH YOUR CHILD THE BASICS OF BODY LANGUAGE

Knowing a few body language tips can give your child an added confidence boost in a new situation. Even if she feels anxious about starting conversations, a simple smile helps

---

* These are friend groups created by teens and based on Elizabeth A. Laugeson, *The Science of Making Friends: Helping Socially Challenged Teens and Young Adults* (San Francisco: Jossey-Bass, 2013).

encourage *others* to make the initial approach. By this point, you've got your SNEAK attack down. For kids, it's even easier. They already know to be Kind, and Neatness doesn't matter as much for them. Kids do need to learn SEA, so we'll focus on the big three: Smiling, Eye contact, and Arms open.

Smiling shows you are nice.
Eye contact shows you are interested.
Arms open shows you are open to making friends.

The most effective way to teach your child about body language is to show her. What does it look like when you use open body language (smiling, making eye contact, and keeping arms open) versus closed (not smiling, avoiding eye contact, and crossing arms)? My favorite way to teach this is through role-playing. At the end of this chapter, I've included scenarios for you to practice at home. After ten minutes, your child will know SEA, and you'll see how silly the situation feels when you *don't* use SEA.

Let your child know that body language isn't only about how others see you. It also affects how we feel about ourselves. Show your child to stand tall and use his power pose.* Do this before heading out on the first day of school: hands on hips, feet apart, head held high, with a big smile. Throw in a man-

---

* There's some debate about the science behind this. I've observed kids who have used the power pose to gain confidence and it works. Whether there's a placebo effect, I have no idea, but I recommend teaching your kids to strike a pose before they face a challenge.

tra he can repeat in his head: "I've got this," or "Today will be a great day." Then, if he ever feels overwhelmed during the school day, he can head to the bathroom and say the mantra to himself in private. In the classroom, he can sit up straight with his shoulders back, give a little smile, and take a deep breath.

PRACTICE ICEBREAKERS TOGETHER

Once your child feels comfortable with SEA, you can teach him how to make the first move. At younger ages, your child can say, "Hi. I'm Ella. What's your name? [Wait for response.] Do you want to play with me?" Teach your child to pause and *listen* to the response. This will be an invaluable, lifelong skill. She should listen, remember the other child's name, and use it often.

For older children, you may need a larger toolbox of conversation starters. *Compliments* are a good place to start:

- "I love your shoes/sweatshirt/lunchbox. Where'd you get it?"
- "Nice shot. Mind if I join you guys?"
- "Cool picture. How'd you draw that?"

Your child can also use her *surroundings* to help her out with conversation topics.

- "Do you know what the homework is? I don't think I got everything."

- "Are you going to the [school event]? I've never been before. Is it fun?"
- "Have you seen that video of [something that's gone viral]? Isn't it crazy?"

When starting a conversation, your child may feel more comfortable using a prop. She could use her phone to say, "Have you seen this new game?" Or she can bring her school assignment book over and say, "Is this the homework for tonight?" Other potential topics include: weekend activities, extracurriculars, celebrities, sports, movies, TV shows, music, books, and current events.

> **To summarize, here are the five steps for how to chat with new friends**
>
> 1. Say hi.
> 2. Make a comment about something (icebreaker).
> 3. Ask a follow-up question to keep the conversation going.
> 4. Introduce yourself.
> 5. Say goodbye using the person's name.

At this point remind your child that these conversations are a way to test the friendship waters. The goal isn't to make a friend right away. The purpose is smaller than that. Your child should aim to talk to a different person each day or to have a longer conversation with one person. That, in and of itself, is a success. Worthwhile friendships take time to build, whether your child is in elementary school or high school. Making friends requires patience and persistence. Remind your child that this is normal and part of the friend-making process.

As much as we hope our daughter meets her BFF on the first day to erase the pain of friends left behind, that's not realistic. She may be sad about her old friends, but she'll feel happy about someone saying "hi" to her on the first day. And that's a great start.

FINALLY, BE A GOOD ROLE MODEL

Your child will look to you for inspiration. Get involved with your community and show your son how it's done. Smile, approach strangers, and try to make friends. If you're lucky, you may meet someone who has a child the same age as yours. If you face rejection, show your child how you handle it with maturity. You can say, "That person couldn't meet me for coffee. I'm a little sad, but I understand that people can be busy with work or their family. I'll ask her again another day, but I'll reach out to other people, too." It's helpful for your child to see that you're going through the same ups and downs.

A QUICK WORD ON TEENAGERS

Moving with a teenager can be difficult. Your teenage child is detaching from you, feeling self-conscious, and going through many changes that have nothing to do with the move. Now, more than ever, your child's life revolves around his friends and potentially his romantic partner. These strong social attachments can make the move especially difficult for him.

To help your teenage child make new friends, give him the space and the privacy that he desires, but also be a friendly face at the end of the day when he needs it. If he's looking for guidance from you, share this book and discuss what you have found to be most useful. Make time to simply listen, to hear what your child is going through, and to be there to validate his feelings. Play basketball or go for a car ride to offer the opportunity for a conversation without forcing it.

On the other hand, if he's not asking for advice, leave this book out on the coffee table. Talk to your spouse or a friend about the friendship chapters at dinnertime and maybe your child will be inclined to pick up the book when no one else is around. Practice the role-playing scenarios with your younger child and see if your teenager wants to join you. If your teenage child is giving you the silent treatment, try not to take it personally. Even if it doesn't seem like he's listening, he probably is. So, try to give him the information he needs to make friends even if you need to be creative about doing so.

ROLE-PLAYING SCENARIOS

Act out the following role-playing scenarios with your child. Some may not seem like they're directly related to making friends, but they cover the main body language tips and conversation talking points. You'll find variations for each scene.

Switch off roles, get an audience (even if it's just some stuffed animals), and take dramatic bows to keep the role-playing silly and light. If you have a live audience, don't tell them what you've changed when you do the variations. Ask if they can spot the differences.

Here are the skills we'll be working on: SEA, conversation starters, saying hi and goodbye, introductions, remembering names, and being kind.

Scene 1: Buying tickets for a movie

In this scene, Kid will *not* smile or make eye contact. Ticket Seller *does* smile and makes eye contact.

KID: Hi. Can I have two tickets to see *The Avengers*?
TICKET SELLER: Sure. Here you go.
KID: Thanks.

VARIATIONS
- Kid smiles.
- Kid makes eye contact.
- Kid says please.

TALKING POINTS
Discussion: Do you notice a difference when someone makes eye contact or smiles? How does it feel different? Did anything

change when polite words were used? Which interaction felt most comfortable to you? Why?

Remember: Smile. Make eye contact. Be polite.

Scene 2: Going to a friend's house

In this scene, Kid arrives at a friend's house. Kid smiles and makes eye contact. Friend's Mom opens the door. She does *not* smile.

KID: Hi, Mrs. Brown. Thanks for having me over.

FRIEND'S MOM: Sure.

KID: Where should I put my jacket?

FRIEND'S MOM: Right there is fine.

KID: Do you know where Chris is?

FRIEND'S MOM: Down in the basement, waiting for you.

KID: Okay, thanks, Mrs. Brown.

VARIATIONS
- Friend's Mom crosses her arms.
- Friend's Mom wears crazy clothes* (no smile).
- Friend's Mom smiles.
- Friend's Mom says Kid's name.

* Get creative here. Put Friend's Mom's shirt on backward, wear socks on hands, or style some crazy hair.

Discussion: What did you think of Friend's Mom? Did she seem welcoming? When she crossed her arms, did she seem more or less friendly? How did you react when you saw her crazy outfit? Did it make you laugh? Did you feel like she was more or less approachable? Did the scene change when Friend's Mom smiled? Did it seem different when she used Kid's name? Which variation did you like the best? Why?

Remember: Smile. Arms open. Be neat. Remember names.

Scene 3: Waiting in line

Kid stands in line to get into school. Student waits next to Kid.

KID: Hi. I like your key chain. Is that the guy from the new Star Wars movie?
STUDENT: Oh, yeah. Thanks. I got it for my birthday.

[Bell rings.]

KID: Bye! See you later.
STUDENT: Bye!

VARIATIONS
- Kid doesn't say "Hi."
- Kid doesn't say "Bye."
- Bell does not ring. Make up rest of conversation.

Discussion: Did the scene change when Kid skipped "Hi" and went straight to the compliment? What was it like when no one said "Bye"? How did the conversation go when you could make it up? Did it feel uncomfortable at first or were you able to have a good conversation?

Remember: Say hi and goodbye. Complimenting others is a good icebreaker.

Scene 4: School locker, day one

Kid and Locker Buddy have lockers right next to each other. They both arrive at their locker at the same time. Kid smiles and makes eye contact.

KID: Hi. I'm Alex. I just moved here last week.

LOCKER BUDDY: Hi, Alex. I'm Sal. Welcome.

KID: Thanks, Sal. Are you in Mrs. Divis's class?

LOCKER BUDDY: No, I have Mr. Sroka, but I heard Mrs. Divis is nice.

KID: Oh, that's good to hear. I should probably head to class now, but I'll see you around, Sal.

LOCKER BUDDY: Yeah. See ya!

VARIATIONS

- Kid doesn't smile.
- Kid doesn't make eye contact.
- Kid crosses his arms.

Discussion: How does the scene change when you don't use SEA? Did you feel more or less comfortable in the original scene or the variations? Why?

Remember: Smile. Eye contact. Arms open. Introduce yourself. Ask a question about your surroundings. End the conversation with an invitation to talk again later.

Scene 5: School locker, continued—day ten

Kid and Locker Buddy make small talk every day. Kid finally feels comfortable enough to take the next step. Kid smiles and makes eye contact.

KID: Hi, Sal. How's it going?

LOCKER BUDDY: Fine. How about you?

KID: Great. I'm excited it's Friday.

LOCKER BUDDY: Me, too!

KID: My mom said I could invite a friend over. Are you free next week?

LOCKER BUDDY: Sure. That sounds fun.

KID: Cool. Want to see if next Tuesday or Friday works for you?

LOCKER BUDDY: Yeah, I'll check with my mom.

KID: Sounds good. Have a good weekend, Sal.

LOCKER BUDDY: Bye, Alex.

- No one remembers names.
- Locker Buddy says he's not available.
- Locker Buddy doesn't say "Bye."

TALKING POINTS

Discussion: How does it feel when you don't use people's names? How did Kid handle it when Locker Buddy said no to his invitation? What are different ways you can deal with someone saying no? Does the conversation feel unfinished when someone doesn't say goodbye?

Remember: Making friends takes time. After talking to the same person for a while, you will get to know him better. Once you feel like you know someone well enough, invite him to do something. You don't need to wait for others to make the first move. If someone says no to your first invitation she may be unavailable at that time. If someone says no several times, then it's time to focus your attention on a new friend.

Practice these role-playing scenarios with your child or let her practice alone in front of a mirror. The more role-playing you do, the easier it will be to handle new social situations.

17

EMBRACING YOUR TOWN

You'll miss the best things if you keep your eyes shut.
—DR. SEUSS, *I Can Read with My Eyes Shut!*

When we moved from Knoxville back to Chicago, there was one thing I was *not* excited about: the weather. As a Florida girl, I was still ill-equipped to handle the seven long months of winter. Seriously, snow in May is just criminal. We moved in January, and determined to welcome the season I feared most, I forced myself past the stacks of unpacked boxes, all the way down to the local ice rink where I signed up for beginner-level ice skating lessons. Unfortunately, the lessons did not include the sparkly outfit I envisioned, but they did teach me to love Chicago (and even its winters) that much more.

DISCOVER WHAT MAKES YOUR NEW PLACE UNIQUE

Remember back in chapter 9 when we talked about your Moving Bucket List? Learning the features of your new town is actually an extension of that. Let's say you've passed the road trip portion and you're semi-settled with your furniture and boxes stashed in your new home. There's no need to unpack everything just yet.

Instead, switch gears and focus on finding out what's

unique about the place where you recently moved. Maybe it's the country music scene or the underground trampoline park in an abandoned coal mine. (I've never been, but I've heard the trampoline park in North Wales in the United Kingdom is rather spectacular.) Whatever the notable attraction of your new area is, explore it. If what makes your city special is a type of cuisine, then try it. Your kitchen won't be unpacked immediately, so give yourself the excuse to visit different restaurants as you get settled. Happiness increases with the *anticipation* of the fun event, so plan for a couple of future activities and mark them on your calendar. It's important to spend some time during your first days and weeks getting out of the house. The unpacking will get done eventually.

TAKE ADVANTAGE OF THE FREE STUFF

When Dan and I lived in Maryland, we would take our folding chairs and a picnic dinner to watch free outdoor movies on the Mall in Washington, D.C. We watched *Roman Holiday* with the backdrop of the Washington Monument, and I couldn't believe that this was our new home and we could do this every week. On weekends we rode our bikes along the Capital Crescent Trail from Bethesda to Georgetown or we hiked in Great Falls Park in Virginia. We didn't need to spend money to enjoy our new city, and we loved living there.

Now that we have kids, our first destination after we move is the library. That wasn't our initial stop when we were in our twenties, but I wish we had recognized back then how much libraries offer. Not only can you check out free physical items—

books, movies, Xbox games—you also get access to digital content such as music, TV shows, and magazines. Plus, some libraries offer passes to local attractions, so you can tour your city for *free*. All you need to do is sign up for a library card.

To find out what other free events are happening around you, sign up for your local newspaper to see its upcoming calendar. Once you discover a venue you like, whether it's a yoga studio or a bookstore, sign up for its newsletter to find out about future events. When you see a concert or a book signing that interests you, pencil it in so you remember to check it out later.

TRY ACTIVITIES OUT OF YOUR COMFORT ZONE

Recently, I spoke with a mom who was moving to Cleveland who had her daughter's activities all figured out. "What about you?" I asked her. "I'll worry about me after we're settled," she told me. And sadly, that's a common moving theme. If you have kids, it's natural to sign them up for activities when you move to a new place. It's rare, though, that people take the same step for themselves.

Back in chapter 13, we talked about forming good habits and how moving is an opportunity for reinvention. Is there something that you've been interested in doing for the first time? Maybe you want to take Zumba classes or apprentice with a chef at a bakery. Yes, I know you're busy with the new job and settling in, but it's worth trying a new activity because it will energize you and help you feel like part of the community. Plus, this is a chance to add excitement and happiness to your life.

After our most recent move back to Chicago, I made a concerted effort to explore different interests. My goal: one new hobby every year. Year one: ice skating. Year two: knitting classes. Year three: guitar lessons. One year seemed like a perfect length of time for the activity to transform from a difficult task to a fun pursuit. You won't see me doing a triple axel anytime soon (or ever), but I can skate around the rink without falling. I'll declare that a success. The exposure to various disciplines became a type of meditation for me. I could appreciate the moment I was in, whether I was learning a folk song or fixing a dropped stitch. Plus, I met some cool people, so it was an all-around win.

WALK AROUND AND DON'T LET PUBLIC TRANSPORTATION INTIMIDATE YOU

Public transit, especially in large cities, can seem intimidating if you don't have to jump in by using it to commute to work right away. My advice? Take the subway or bus within the first two weeks of your arrival. If you live in the suburbs and there's a commuter rail, take it into town. Prove to yourself that you can learn the system so that you'll make good on that promise to go downtown on weekends.

While public transit is a good way to travel over long distances, the best way to get to know a city is by going for a walk. You may come across an antique furniture store or a Mexican restaurant that you'd never notice if you drove by it.

Dan and I discovered our favorite movie theater in Palo Alto, California, after we explored the area on foot. The theater advertised its Mighty Wurlitzer organ that would play before the movie started and during intermissions. We decided to buy two tickets. A throwback to classic Hollywood with its red curtains and an organist, the theater delivered. We loved the atmosphere as the audience cheered on Jimmy Stewart in *Mr. Smith Goes to Washington.* If we had looked for movie options online, we would've picked the latest blockbuster and we would have missed this memorable experience. Walking around town can help you find the hidden gems.

INVITE FRIENDS TO VISIT

You know what it's like when friends come to visit. All of a sudden you turn into a professional tour guide, taking them to the Statue of Liberty and the Empire State Building and Ellen's Stardust Diner so they can experience the singing waitstaff in Times Square. You go to places you would never go on your own, and—surprisingly—you have a lot of fun. To make the visit even more interesting for both you and your guests, learn a few facts about your city before they arrive. That way you can share what's cool about where you live, and you'll feel more invested in your community.

If you're like my husband, you might learn about Al Capone and the various Mafia crime scenes scattered about Chicago. When friends come to visit us, their VIP tour goes something like this:

DAN: Anyone remember Hymie Weiss, "the only man Al Capone ever feared"? Yeah, well, Al Capone's boys mowed him down on the steps of that cathedral right there. You can still see a bullet hole from the Tommy Guns in the cornerstone—

ALI: And that's the Magnificent Mile right over there.

Needless to say, there's more than one way to share your new town. You might focus on your favorite restaurants or revel in the . . . *colorful* history of the area.

LET THE KIDS PLAN FUN ACTIVITIES, TOO

If you're moving with kids, this is an ideal opportunity to give your children some control. Brainstorm places to visit together or let your son or daughter pick a day where he or she plans the family's activities. Give your child access to a guidebook, online maps, review sites, and a budget. Since anticipation is a big part of the fun, allow a few days or weeks of planning time—even if it's before you move.

By now you've learned how to form good habits that will make you happier, build a community from scratch, create a happy home filled with objects and people you love, and get to know your city. Now it's time for a few final tips to get you to your happily ever after.

18

_____

THE HAPPILY EVER AFTER
CHECKLIST

*The main thing is to be moved, to love, to hope, to tremble,
to live.*

—AUGUSTE RODIN

I've interviewed many people about their moves, and some
moves without question are harder than others. Wherever
your move falls on the spectrum, there's no getting around
the fact that moving is tough. There's no amount of preparation that will totally spare you the challenges of this process.
But with the right mental and emotional (and occasionally
snack-oriented) tool kits, you can make the transition easier.

The truth is, there are as many secrets to Happy Moving
as there are to happy living, bits of wisdom large and small.
Some work for some people, others work for others. I don't pretend to have all the answers, but I do know what works for me
and my family, and these tricks have gotten us through many
seasons of change. Earlier in the book I explained my Happy
Moving tips—declutter, declutter, declutter!—and in this chapter I offer some general advice for the living happily ever after the move part. Let's start with my final, all-encompassing,
Happy Moving checklist.

The Happily Ever After Checklist

1. Focus on the people in your life.
2. Be kind.
3. Be grateful.
4. Choose the path *you* want.
5. Be happy for other people.
6. Recognize that piles of money won't make you happier.
7. Go outside every day.
8. Take vacations.
9. Think of the activities that make you happy and do them.
10. Watch TV and screens . . . for a little while.
11. Buy experiences instead of possessions.
12. Make the most of the time you have.
13. Avoid long commutes.
14. Find your purpose at work.
15. Play often
16. Tell people how much you love them.
17. Give more hugs.
18. Savor a home-cocked meal.
19. Exercise every day.
20. Eat ice cream.

1. FOCUS ON THE PEOPLE IN YOUR LIFE.

I write about friendships and creating a community because every book on happiness will tell you that social relationships form the foundation of a happy human existence. Regardless of your desires, accomplishments, or sufferings, in the end it's the people you care for and your interactions with them that matter most. So, spend time with your loved ones and focus on making new friends. Call your family. Email or write a letter to your friends who still live back where you used to live. Meet up for coffee with someone from work or go for a run with a running group. Smile at a neighbor. So much of this book is about connecting with others because our relationships with friends, family, and even strangers provide us with the human contact we need to be happy.

2. BE KIND.

Kindness is everything. When Dan and I moved from California to Chicago, I needed to fly out early to start my job as a summer intern at a law firm. We shipped our Honda Passport while Dan drove a U-Haul truck across the country with his brother, Steven. For reasons that are still unclear, the transport company said they couldn't bring the car into Chicago, and that I needed to wire them more money before they disclosed the car's location. I feared for our poor Honda, blindfolded and held hostage in an unknown place.

Thankfully, one of the lawyers at the firm came to my rescue. Not only did Charles discover the whereabouts of our car, he drove me an hour and a half outside the city to reclaim it. Without his help, I don't know what I would've done—alone in a new city without my car or a way to get it back. One small act can make a huge difference in someone else's life. I'm thankful for the kindness shown to me, and I try to pay it forward. Be kind. Kindness begets kindness.

3. BE GRATEFUL.

If you want to be happy, appreciate what you have. Take a minute to think about what you have at this moment. Who has helped you during this process? What new experiences await you? You would not have gotten to where you are now if it weren't for the events of the past, and all of these combined experiences will help you continue to grow and learn. When you feel grateful for the opportunity presented to you by this move, you will also find joy.

4. CHOOSE THE PATH *YOU* WANT.

It is my hope that you are choosing or have chosen to move because of the things that are most important to you, as we discussed in chapter 1. If so, your move will be the first step down a path toward a full and vital life. Continue to walk down that path by choosing to live intentionally with your priorities in order. Whatever you choose to do with your life, follow the route that aligns with who you are—your desires and your long-term goals. Be you. You'll be happier that way.

5. BE HAPPY FOR OTHER PEOPLE.

When life is hard or we're in the throes of moving, we may feel jealous of people who seem settled or happy. For your own happiness, though, resist the temptation to be envious of others. Giving in to envy is the best way to suck the joy out of life. There will always be someone richer, funnier, or better looking. We can choose to fixate on what others have and condemn ourselves to a life of misery. Or we can choose to celebrate our own successes regardless of what's happening in the lives of the people around us. Recognize your own version of awesome, whatever it is you're moving toward right now, and live that life with confidence. Do that first, and you'll find it's much easier to be happy, *genuinely* happy, when good things happen to the people in your life. Sharing in their successes will contribute to your own happiness as well.

6. RECOGNIZE THAT PILES OF MONEY WON'T MAKE YOU HAPPIER.

The financial rat race may be one reason that people feel envious of others, but research shows that our happiness increases only until we hit an annual income level of $75,000 and then it plateaus. Making more than $75,000 doesn't make our happiness go up at all. In fact, some research has found that the ability to appreciate life's simple pleasures, and therefore to feel happier, may actually go down at annual income levels higher than $75,000. Even more telling than how much we make is how much we owe.[*] So, keep your happiness in mind before you take out a mortgage that's larger than you can afford.

[*] Elizabeth Dunn and Michael Norton, *Happy Money: The Science of Happier Spending* (New York: Simon & Schuster, 2013), p. 95.

7. GO OUTSIDE EVERY DAY.

Being around nature makes us happier. That's why it's important to choose a home that allows you to walk to a nearby park or that provides opportunities to feel the sun on your face in the morning. If you can, make the effort to bike around the neighborhood or tend to a community garden. My husband works in a dark, windowless room in the bowels of a hospital, which worries me because I know how critical contact with nature is to our happiness. I help Dan by encouraging evening walks, or I might remind him how crucial mowing the lawn is to his health . . . because that's the kind of loving wife that I am.

8. TAKE VACATIONS.

After you've settled into your home, start planning for a future vacation—even if it's a year down the road. The reason to start planning now is that a significant portion of the joy of a trip comes from anticipating it. So, even if you aren't able to go on the vacation quite yet, it's good to dream about it. Once you are settled and you've budgeted for a trip, consider making it an eight-day vacay. That's the length of time one study found to be ideal for maximizing your vacation happiness.[*]

[*] J. de Bloom, S. A. E Geurts, and M. A. J. Kompier, "Vacation (After-) Effects on Employee Health and Well-Being, and the Role of Vacation Activities, Experiences and Sleep," *Journal of Happiness Studies*, 14(2013): p. 613. https://doi.org/10.1007/s10902-012-9345-3.

9. THINK OF THE ACTIVITIES THAT MAKE YOU HAPPY AND DO THEM.

When we lived in Knoxville, I couldn't run to the beach. Now that we live in Chicago again, I feel grateful every time I run to Lake Michigan. I never appreciated the easy access to the beach before we moved away. Each one of our moves has taught me something about myself—from my love of the beach to how vitally important my friends are to me. Hopefully, you've discovered your own hidden joys while reading this book. Once you know what you like, incorporate it into your daily life. Appreciate it. Make a habit of doing the things you love.

10. WATCH TV AND SCREENS . . . FOR A LITTLE WHILE.

Scary fact for you: Every day, the average American spends over eleven hours consuming media. According to the 2018 Nielsen Report, we devote more than four and a half hours of that time to television, and we spend another two hours and twenty minutes on our smartphones.[*] Yet, we spend only 39 minutes socializing with friends.[†] Friends make us happier than screens, so we should probably work on evening up these numbers a bit. There's nothing wrong with wanting to

[*] The Nielsen Report, Q1 2018.

[†] American Time Use Survey, Bureau of Labor Statistics, https://www.bls.gov/tus/a1_2017.pdf.

watch a movie, play video games, or scroll through Twitter. But it's also important to set boundaries for yourself so you can engage in activities that nurture you, like playing cards with friends or meeting someone for dinner after work.

11. BUY EXPERIENCES INSTEAD OF POSSESSIONS.

If you have decluttering on your mind, the idea of accumulating more items probably exhausts you. But one day after your move, you will forget that feeling and the Amazon boxes will appear on your doorstep again. Of course, there will be *some* items that you'll need, but the rest . . . ? That pair of cute shoes or your new label maker will give you an initial happy buzz, but the novelty will soon wear off.

Experiences, on the other hand, *do* make us happier—especially if they bring us together with other people. Shared experiences create bonds, so invite people to brunch at your house or ask someone to join you for a movie. Experiences you do alone will also add to your happiness. Think about what you want on your life résumé. Watercolor lessons, skydiving, mastering the game rooms around town? This is your life, so live it.

12. MAKE THE MOST OF THE TIME YOU HAVE.

Time is the most precious thing we have. Use it wisely before and after your move. Batch errands together geographically and pick one day to do them instead of going to Target on Monday, the post office on Tuesday, and the Department of Motor Vehicles on Wednesday. Do some meal planning so you can grocery shop in one trip instead of making a decision every night about what's for dinner. Carpool with families in the neighborhood to get the kids to their activities. Focus your time and energy on the people and activities that enrich your life. When you use your time efficiently, you create the time you need to do the activities that you enjoy.

13. AVOID LONG COMMUTES.

Speaking of wasting time, commuting is *the* happiness killer and yet it doesn't get as much press as it should. The following warning label should be placed on every car, bus, and mass transit train:

Excessive commutes kill happiness.

What is the effect of a long commute on your happiness meter? It's bad.

This is what the research shows: If you commute one hour each way, you would need to earn 40 percent more to achieve the same level of happiness as someone who walks to work.[*] If we scale this in emotional terms instead of a dollar amount, when compared to the commuter, the walker rates his happi-

[*] Charles Montgomery, *Happy City: Transforming Our Lives Through Urban Design* (New York: Farrar, Straus, and Giroux, 2013), p. 83.

ness the same as someone who recently fell in love.* Now, *that's* happy. Okay, well, what about the spouses of these hour-long commuters? Does accepting a longer commute make for a happier family? Not according to the research. "If anything," Elizabeth Dunn and Michael Norton state, "people report somewhat lower happiness when their spouse has a longer commute."†

Why, then, do people suffer through long commutes? The better house, the greener lawn, the cost of living? Maybe. The question is whether those things make the commute worth it to you. Maybe you have no choice, or maybe in your case that "bigger house" means having a bedroom for each child. If you *do* have a choice really think about your commute before you commit to a home. If you've already committed to a place to live, see if you can drive during off-peak hours to decrease your commute time. Or consider taking the train at the same time as your friends or carpool with coworkers so you can socialize during this time (even if it's just once a week).

14. FIND YOUR PURPOSE AT WORK.

You'll look at the world from a fresh perspective when you move, so use this time to reframe the way you look at your profession. It turns out that people feel happier when they feel a sense of purpose both in life and in their work. So, find the merits of your job. Instead of looking at your profession as a means to a paycheck, think about how you make someone

* Ibid.

† Dunn and Norton, *Happy Money*, p. 64.

else's day better. If you work at the dry cleaners, you provide customers with clean clothes so they look respectable. If you work at a dentist's office, you help people feel more confident about their smile. Whatever your job is, you impact others and you make a difference. Focus on your purpose instead of on the menial daily tasks that are part of the workday and you will feel happier.

15. PLAY OFTEN.

Whether you're decluttering to move or in the process of unpacking, take a moment and set aside the serious tasks. Just play. Be silly. Dance at home with the lights off and the music blasting. Draw a picture. Bake cookies. Blow bubbles. Pick up a dandelion and make a wish. Then, after you move, remember that you moved for a better life, so you could enjoy yourself. Get on a bike (and not at a spin class). Build a sandcastle. Dig a hole. Roll down a hill. Skip. Color. Do a jigsaw puzzle. Build a model airplane. Put on too much makeup and throw on a boa. Go sledding. Seek out people who make you laugh. Watch more cat videos. Fly a kite. Finger-paint. Splash in the ocean. Enjoy life.

16. TELL PEOPLE HOW MUCH YOU LOVE THEM.

When you are saying goodbye to family and friends in preparation for your move, tell them you love them. While you're feeling sentimental, write a thank-you note to a friend and be specific about *why* you appreciate them. If your friend supported you when you lost your job or when you made the decision to move, tell her how much that meant to you. Then, continue to show your appreciation for the ones you love after you move. Thank your partner for taking out the trash or folding the laundry. A quick text or a note tucked under a pillow will make both you and the other person feel happier.

17. GIVE MORE HUGS.

People need human connection, especially during trying times like moving. I'd say one of my most important roles in helping people through their moves is to be there for them with both a hug and a smile as I listen to their stories. In general, a handshake, a pat on the back, or even a touch on the arm can improve your well-being and help you feel less stressed. So, reach out to a friend with a kind touch, but be aware of relevant cultural norms and people's personal space.

I grew up in Miami, where everyone greets each other with a hug and a kiss on the cheek. The day after I returned from a trip to Miami, I spotted another preschool mom at a grocery store in Chicago. Even though I barely knew her I gave her a big hug and a kiss and asked, "How's your summer going?" She stepped back, said, "Great!" and looked for the nearest exit. I'm pretty sure that's the last time we hung out. Yes, personal space is important.

18. SAVOR A HOME-COOKED MEAL.

During the days leading up to your move and probably the weeks after, you won't be cooking at home much. Once you get settled in, though, make time for a home-cooked meal. If you don't know how to cook, learn one simple recipe. Then, invite someone over and enjoy the meal together. Good food and drink are some of life's greatest pleasures.

19. EXERCISE EVERY DAY.

Exercise gives you endorphins. Endorphins make you happy.
Happy people just don't shoot their husbands. They just don't.

—ELLE WOODS, in *Legally Blonde*

Enough said.

20. EAT ICE CREAM.

One part of our family motto is: "Ice cream makes everything better." Ice cream has gotten us through some difficult moves and we also use it to celebrate life's great moments. My advice to you: find your ice cream.

19

YOU'VE GOT THIS

When you focus on the goodness in your life, you create more of it.

—OPRAH WINFREY, *What I Know For Sure*

There've been times during our moves when I've cried. Like that time we were loading our U-Haul truck in Ohio and our belongings almost didn't fit. Or that time our Knoxville home spent months on the market without a showing. That was stressful. And of course, saying goodbye to friends time and again hasn't been easy.

But you know what? We made it through. And so did every single person I interviewed for this book. And so will you. It takes a strong person to make a big change in life and *you* are that strong person. Think of everything you've already accomplished to get to the point where you are now.

BE KIND TO YOURSELF

When Dan and I were in the process of selling our first home, Dan would take our two toddlers to Potbelly's while I, with baby Charlotte in the BabyBjörn carrier, met with Realtors. After the showings, I'd join my family for chocolate milkshakes.

It didn't matter that it was the third time that week we went out for shakes or that weekend showings also segued into trips to the donut shop. We did what we needed to do to maintain our sanity. And I'm pretty sure that's why our kids love it when we sell a house.

Remember to treat yourself after a day of packing or meeting with moving companies to get estimates. Look back at your bucket list from chapter 9 and do some of the activities that bring you happiness with the people you love.

Practice self-compassion

Moving stirs up a multitude of emotions, perhaps because we reminisce about the past and contemplate the future. Or maybe it's because we're exhausted, and we need more snacks. During this emotional time, you may think negative thoughts like "I'm never going to finish packing before my lease is up" or "I've made the entire family miserable because of my new job." Recognize how often you make negative comments and try to stop yourself from saying them. Instead, say kind statements like "Go me! I packed my books in an hour" or "I'm giving our family the best opportunity I can." Talk to yourself as if your best friend were talking to you and tell yourself how much you are doing right—because you *are* doing a lot of things right.

Practice gratitude

Use a gratitude journal or a gratitude jar to jot down notes to yourself every day during the move. In our house, we write on scraps of paper that we put into a brown paper lunch bag with a smiley face on it. Once you have your gratitude journal of choice, write down the reasons you are grateful and challenge yourself to come up with a different reason each time, such as "I'm grateful my friend stopped by with cookies today" or "I'm grateful I sold my recliner." Read through your journal whenever you feel less than enthusiastic about the move.

PAY IT FORWARD, ONCE YOU FEEL SETTLED

I have no doubt that you are about to or have just aced this move. You've decluttered like Marie Kondo was watching. You've packed the truck with the precision of an engineer. And once you get to where you're going, you'll be surrounded by new friends in no time. So, since you have everything covered, I would like to ask a favor of you: please pay your moving kindness forward by being nice to the next new kid. Read on for some inspiration on how to do so.

Welcome your neighbor

When you see a moving truck, that's your cue. No, it's not your cue to laugh and think, "Thank goodness that's not me!" (Although I may have thought that on occasion . . .) Head over and introduce yourself. Bring a take-out menu from your favorite local restaurant or a batch of blueberry muffins. Leave a note with your name and contact information so the neighbor can reach you if she needs anything.

Invite the new person for coffee

If someone recently moved into your apartment building, invite her to coffee so you can answer questions about the area and help her feel welcome. Breaking the ice is tough, and people will appreciate it when you take the first step.

Be inclusive

Maybe you've settled into a book club or a tennis league. Now that you have a group of friends, you may be hesitant to change your routine. Try to remember what a huge difference it would've made if someone had included *you* when you first arrived. Be the person who includes others. If the invitation to a regular activity is too much of a commitment for someone you don't know well, include the new arrival in a girls' night out or a special event where she can hang out with a group for the night.

Start up a welcoming committee in your community

If your workplace or your kid's school doesn't have a welcoming procedure for newcomers, start up your own. Give the new guy the office tour on his first day of work and give him a list of the best lunch places near the office. Set up a family match program for incoming families at school and include a list of reliable babysitters. Those parents will be eternally grateful.

Thank you, movers and readers, for spending your time with me. Now, go get to work. I hear you have some decluttering to do. Happy Moving!

ACKNOWLEDGMENTS

Happy Moving. What a concept, right? Without my incredible agent, Jenny Herrera, moving would still just be a miserable experience. Thank you, Jenny, for believing.

I am grateful to Emma Brodie, a masterful editor who shaped my ideas into this book. Thank you, Emma, for your invaluable insight and for making me smile each time I read your notes. I loved working on this book with you.

It has been a privilege to work with the brilliant team at William Morrow, including Liate Stehlik, Benjamin Steinberg, Cassie Jones, Susan Kosko, Fritz Metsch, Mumtaz Mustafa, Shelby Peak, Bianca Flores, and Lauren Lauzon. Thank you also to Lise Sukhu, my illustrator, for the happiest cover art I could imagine and for including my mom's cat, Bocelli.

I owe thanks to all the people who shared their moving stories with me, the families that have attended my workshops, my blog readers, and the readers of this book. You inspire me and I love learning from you.

Moving has deepened my gratitude for friendship, and I've been blessed with the world's best. First and foremost, Marisa Guarino, for making me laugh since we were four years old. To the Miami crew, the Lowell 8-Women, and my Chicago friends: thank you for the laughter, the late-night chats, and the dance parties.

To my parents, John and Lucia; my brother, John; and my

grandmother, Josefina, for inspiring me to explore new places and to enjoy life. It's also hard to imagine my life without the enormous and welcoming family I married into. Thank you to Kathy and Frank, and to (in Christmas line order) Jenny, David, Susan, Mary, Jeff, Steven, Robyn, Jen, Anton, John, Josh, and all my amazing nieces and nephews.

To Victoria, Joseph, and Charlotte: Thank you for the hugs, chocolate chip cookies, and notes of encouragement while I hid away to write this book. I love you with all of my heart.

To my husband, my moving partner, my first editor, and my best friend, Daniel: I love you. I couldn't have done any of this without you. Truly. Those moving boxes can get really heavy.

APPENDIX

MOVING CHECKLIST

8 Weeks Before: Get Organized

- ❑ Set a moving date.
- ❑ Create a filing system for all moving papers: estimates, receipts, health and school records.
- ❑ Tell family and friends about your move.
- ❑ Get in-home moving estimates from at least three moving companies for both moving and packing.
- ❑ Notify your landlord.
- ❑ Set up appointments with your doctor, dentist, veterinarian, and hairstylist.
- ❑ Begin collecting free packing supplies from sites such as Craigslist and Nextdoor.
- ❑ Back up important files on your computer.

6 Weeks Before: Declutter and Consider Pet Travel

- ❑ Go over the floor plan of your new home.
- ❑ If the furniture doesn't fit in your new home, plan to donate it or sell it.
- ❑ Begin decluttering your belongings (the sooner, the better).
- ❑ Take pet(s) to vet for vaccinations, health records, and certificates.

- ❑ Make travel reservations and contact hotels and/or airlines regarding pet accommodations.
- ❑ Contact the Department of Motor Vehicles for new driver's license(s) and registration forms.
- ❑ Contact your insurance agent for coverage both during and after your move.
- ❑ Establish a bank account in your new location. Do not close local accounts yet.

4 Weeks Before: Confirm Moving Arrangements

- ❑ Book a moving company or rent your own moving van. Weekends and holidays book quickly.
- ❑ Decide whether to ship or drive your car. If shipping, make arrangements.
- ❑ Research parking issues for the moving truck for both sides of the move. Do you need a parking permit?
- ❑ Can a large moving truck easily navigate around your neighborhood to reach your home and/or storage facility, or will a small moving van be required to shuttle your belongings to/from the larger truck?
- ❑ Hire a babysitter for moving day.
- ❑ Contact utility companies and delivery services regarding turn-off and turn-on dates.
- ❑ Arrange for school records to be transferred to your new school district.
- ❑ Buy moving supplies such as boxes, tape, box cutters, bubble wrap, and permanent markers.

3 Weeks Before: Pack Up and Change Your Address

- ❑ Start packing. The earlier you start, the more organized you'll be. Label everything.
- ❑ Set up farewell parties with family and friends at a local park or restaurant.
- ❑ Plan a garage sale or finish donating items you no longer need.
- ❑ Do car maintenance.
- ❑ Arrange for mail forwarding with the U.S. Post Office.
- ❑ Schedule appointments with real estate agents or landlords for key exchange for old and new residences.
- ❑ Hire a landscaping service for after your move if your house is not sold yet.
- ❑ Notify important parties (see Change of Address Notification Checklist on page 235).

You're doing amazing. Keep it up!

2 Weeks Before: Last-Minute Errands

- ❑ Set up utilities, cable, and home security for your new location.
- ❑ Return all borrowed items to the library or friends.
- ❑ Pick up any remaining items from the dry cleaners.
- ❑ Arrange for hazardous waste pickup of old paint cans or gas drained from your power equipment.
- ❑ Find homes for plants and/or pets you cannot take with you.
- ❑ Reconfirm dates for packing, pickup, and delivery with your moving company.

- ❏ Settle any outstanding bills.
- ❏ Contact your child's new school to arrange a visit prior to the first day of school, if possible.

Moving Week: Eat Chocolate and Other Perishable Goods

- ❏ Create a Moving Day Survival Kit, which includes box cutters, Sharpies, snacks, and games for kids.
- ❏ Consider purchasing or renting a furniture dolly or hand truck to help you on both sides of the move.
- ❏ Pack a suitcase for your travels.
- ❏ Pack everything except essential items and use paper plates and disposable utensils.
- ❏ Give perishable food to family or friends.
- ❏ Refill prescriptions.
- ❏ Empty your freezer, clean it, and dry it out for at least twenty-four hours before moving day.
- ❏ Pack Need Immediately boxes, which may include a coffee maker, toilet paper, and light bulbs.
- ❏ Enjoy a night out with the people you'll miss the most.

Moving Day: Survival Mode and Bribery

- ❏ Bribe loved ones to help you pack up the truck.
- ❏ If possible, take kids or pets to a family member's or friend's house for the day.
- ❏ If using movers, oversee the inventory list as well as the packing and loading process.
- ❏ Before the movers leave, do a sweep of your home to make sure nothing was left behind.

- ❑ Clean your home so you don't lose your rental deposit.
- ❑ Meet with your landlord to review the checkout form and receive a refund agreement.
- ❑ Leave your keys with your landlord, your real estate agent, or the buyers.
- ❑ Celebrate that you survived!

You did it! Congratulations. May you live happily ever after in your new home.

CHANGE OF ADDRESS NOTIFICATION CHECKLIST

PEOPLE AND COMPANIES TO NOTIFY	CONTACT INFORMATION
Accountant	
Alarm company	
Babysitter	
Bank	
Cable TV provider	
Car loan	

PEOPLE AND COMPANIES TO NOTIFY	CONTACT INFORMATION
Cell phone service provider	
Consumer loans	
Credit card companies	
Credit union	
Daycare	
Dentist	
Department of Motor Vehicles	
Doctor	
Dry cleaners	
Electric company	
Employer	
Family and friends	

PEOPLE AND COMPANIES TO NOTIFY	CONTACT INFORMATION
Frequent flier cards	
Gas company	
Government benefits	
Insurance	
• Car	
• Disability	
• Health	
• Home	
• Life	
• Property	
Internet service provider	
Investment firms	

Best of luck on your move. You're rockin' it!

PEOPLE AND COMPANIES TO NOTIFY	CONTACT INFORMATION
IRS (Form 8822)	1-800-TAX-FORM
Landlord	
Landscaping company	
Magazines	
Mortgage company	
Newspaper	
Passport office	
Post office	
Professional organizations	
Property tax office	
Religious organizations	

PEOPLE AND COMPANIES TO NOTIFY	CONTACT INFORMATION
School	
Social Security Administration	1-800-772-1213
Taxes	
• Federal (See IRS)	
• State	
• Local	
Trash and recycling	
Tutor	
Veterinarian	
Voter registration	
Water/sewer company	

MOVING RESOLUTIONS

I'm using my clean slate to make some changes.

THE NEW ME	MAKING IT HAPPEN	GOAL DATE	ACHIEVED?

MOVING RESOLUTIONS SAMPLE

THE NEW ME	MAKING IT HAPPEN	GOAL DATE	ACHIEVED?
Arrives to work ten minutes early.	**1.** Get things ready night beforehand.	Achieved if done every day for one week.	❏
	2. Set clocks forward to trick myself about time.	Achieved if changed clocks.	❏
Exercises two times per week.	**1.** Walk one mile on Sunday evening and Wednesday morning.	Walking goal achieved at end of two weeks.	❏
	2. Join gym to meet new people.	Achieved if join gym one week after move.	❏
Tries new things.	**1.** Take an evening adult class.	Achieved if signed up one month after move.	❏
	2. Try one new restaurant each month.	Achieved if tried new place by 15th of the month.	❏

QUESTIONS TO ASK BEFORE YOU HIRE A MOVER

Tell me about yourself

1. Can I please set up an in-home estimate?
2. Do you offer binding or "not to exceed" estimates? (You want to avoid nonbinding estimates.)
3. Are you the moving company I will be working with or are you a broker?
4. Do you subcontract your moves?
5. Can I please get your licensing information?
6. What services does your estimate include?
7. What services are *not* included?
8. What paperwork will you provide to me?

   Forms you should receive:
   - moving estimate
   - bill of lading (i.e., your moving contract)
   - inventory list (aka cube sheet or table of measurements)
   - Your Rights and Responsibilities When You Move pamphlet

9. Can you please provide me with three references from former customers?

Damaged items

1. What kind of liability coverage do you provide?
2. How do you prevent property damage?
3. How do you handle missing or damaged items?

Moving logistics

1. Are there restrictions on what I can pack?
2. Who will handle parking permits or elevator restrictions?
3. How long will the move take?
4. How can I contact you or the driver during the move?
5. Who will handle the arrival portion of my move?
6. When will my items arrive?
7. What if my items arrive before I do?
8. Are there storage facilities available?

Fees

1. How much will my move cost?
2. Do you offer any discounts?
3. Do you require a deposit? If so, how much is it?
4. What is your cancellation policy?
5. What do you consider additional services to be and how much do you charge for them?
6. Will additional transfers be required from a smaller truck to a larger truck due to parking or space restrictions?
7. What additional fees am I not aware of?

Other

1. Do you work with Move for Hunger so I can donate my nonperishable food?
2. Do you have any questions for me?

QUESTIONS TO ASK BEFORE YOU HIRE A REALTOR

General questions

1. Do you specialize in certain neighborhoods?
2. How well do you know the local area?
3. Do you specialize in a certain price range?
4. How long have you been working as a real estate agent?
5. What is your schedule like?
6. Are you available days, nights, and weekends?
7. Do you work as part of a team?
8. How many clients are you working with currently?
9. What percentage of your business is helping buyers versus sellers?
10. How much do you charge?
11. Is that fee negotiable?
12. Do you have a list of other professionals you recommend (lawyers, mortgage brokers, home inspectors, etc.)? If so, can you please provide me with their names?
13. What are the closing costs?
14. What's the best way to communicate with you (phone, text, email, in person)?
15. Can you please provide three references?

For buyers

1. How will you help me find my dream home?
2. How many buyers have you worked with in the last year?

3. How long does it take your buyers to find and purchase a home?
4. How do you resolve conflicts? For example, what if I want to buy a house and you represent the seller or if another buyer you represent wants the same house?
5. What neighborhood would you recommend to your best friend?

For sellers

1. How do you plan to market my home, and is a free analysis from a professional staging company included?
2. Can I please have a written comparative market analysis of homes on the market?
3. How many days on average are your listings on the market?
4. What is your sale-to-list ratio?
5. How long does the listing contract last?

MOVING DAY SURVIVAL KIT

These items will help you make it through moving day:

- ❑ Food, water, and snacks
- ❑ Disposable dishware and cups
- ❑ Box cutters, scissors, and Band-Aids
- ❑ Sharpies, Ziploc bags, packing tape, and rubber bands
- ❑ Furniture dolly
- ❑ Furniture pads or covers
- ❑ Bungee cords and plastic wrap
- ❑ Ratchet tie-down straps or nylon rope
- ❑ Toilet paper
- ❑ Garbage bags
- ❑ Vacuum or Swiffer and a dustpan
- ❑ Hand soap
- ❑ A sense of humor

MOVING DAY SURVIVAL KIT FOR KIDS

To help your kids make it through moving day, keep these items handy:

- ❑ Snacks and candy
- ❑ Water bottles
- ❑ Electronic devices
- ❑ Favorite toy or blanket
- ❑ Coloring pads
- ❑ Playing cards

- ❏ Folding chairs or some place to sit
- ❏ Clear plastic bin with favorite belongings packed in car

MOVING DAY SURVIVAL KIT FOR PETS

Don't forget your furry friend. Keep her happy with:

- ❏ Food, snacks, treats, and bottled water
- ❏ Food bowl (disposable if you prefer)
- ❏ A secure, well-ventilated crate
- ❏ An airline-approved carrier
- ❏ Favorite toys
- ❏ Litter box or absorbent travel pet pads, paper towels, and wipes
- ❏ ID tags with your new address, leash, and collar
- ❏ Vet records and medications

NEED IMMEDIATELY BOX(ES)

The contents will vary based on your individual needs and desires, but here are some ideas to get you started. Place this box (or boxes) in the truck last so you can get to it *immediately*.

- ❏ Disposable dishware
- ❏ Picnic blanket
- ❏ Toilet paper
- ❏ Paper towels
- ❏ Cleaning supplies for your old place and your new one

- ❑ Garbage bags
- ❑ A lamp (or two)
- ❑ Light bulbs
- ❑ Clock
- ❑ Flashlights and batteries
- ❑ Hand and bath towels
- ❑ Soap
- ❑ Toiletries
- ❑ Pillow
- ❑ Air mattress, sleeping bag, and blanket
- ❑ Band-Aids and Tylenol
- ❑ Coffee maker, coffee filters, ground coffee, and sugar packets

ITEMS YOU WILL PROBABLY KEEP WITH YOU IN THE CAR/TRUCK

- ❑ House keys
- ❑ Cell phone and charger
- ❑ Electronic devices
- ❑ Identification
- ❑ Folder of important paperwork

DONATION VALUE GUIDE

Everyone's financial situation is different and tax laws change, so *please* check with a tax advisor to determine whether you should itemize your donations. As a general rule, it's worth itemizing your charitable donations if your itemized deduction is greater than your standardized deduction.

To get an idea of what donated items are worth, take a quick look at the following chart to see how your decluttering efforts can add up. If you use a tax software program, you will find more details for each item. For example, did you donate a woman's long-sleeve blouse or a woman's T-shirt? The software will make it easy for you to choose the correct item as long as you keep a detailed record of the items you donate. Values vary based on the age and quality of the item.

DONATION VALUE GUIDE

WOMEN'S CLOTHING	TAX DEDUCTIBLE VALUE
Bathrobe	$3–$12
Blouse	$3–$12
Two-piece suit	$6–$96
Sweater	$4–$15
Pants	$4–$25
Evening dress	$6–$60
Handbag	$2–$20
Shoes	$2–$30
MEN'S CLOTHING	
Jacket	$8–$25
Suit	$5–$96
Shorts	$4–$10
Shirt	$3–$12
Shoes	$3–$30
Pants	$4–$23

CHILDREN'S CLOTHING

Shirt	$2-$10
Sweater	$2-$10
Jeans	$2-$12
Snowsuit	$2-$19

FURNITURE

Sofa	$35-$395
Bed	$35-$170
Mattress	$13-$75
Dining room set	$150-$900
Coffee table	$15-$100
Table lamp	$3-$75

DREAM HOME WISH LIST

Write down the basics for your ideal place, such as the number of bedrooms or bathrooms. Now's your chance to dream big. What do you want in your new home?

Rent or buy? _____

Size: # of bedrooms _____   # of bathrooms _____

Ideal neighborhood(s): _____

Now for the DREAM BIG portion. (There's a sample mind map for you on the next page if you want some inspiration.)

If you want to create your own mind map, set a timer for five minutes. Write "My Dream Home" in the middle. Then, jot down five wish list items that come to mind. Circle them. Then, create circles based off those circles and keep filling in the circles until time is up. When you're done, go back to see if any words or ideas come up several times. Maybe it's "sunny" or "friends" or "quiet." Make that characteristic a priority when you shop for your dream home.

WHAT DOES YOUR DREAM HOME LOOK LIKE?

- Guest space
- Sunny master bedroom
- Bedroom for kids
- 3 Bedrooms
- Lots of windows
- MUST HAVE LIGHT!
- Sunny
- Bright happy colors
- My Dream Home
- Sidewalks
- Walkable
- Close to Parks
- Green space
- Close to downtown
- Lincoln Park
- Things to do
- Good schools
- Open Floor Plan
- Place to entertain
- Kitchen opens to living space
- Space for family to gather

CREATE YOUR HAPPY HOME ROOM BY ROOM

....

How will you use the room?

Do you have an oasis for yourself in the room?

Will you be able to entertain in the space?

What makes the room special?

Can you highlight the unique features?

Does the room appeal to all of your senses?

Do you feel happy in the room?

....
MASTER BEDROOM
....

Paint color: _____

Accessories color: _____

Favorite items: _____

Special nook: _____

Lighting: _____

Storage: _____

Sensory appeal: _____

MASTER BATHROOM

Paint color: _____

Accessories color: _____

Favorite items: _____

Lighting: _____

Storage: _____

Sensory appeal: _____

CHILD'S BEDROOM

Paint color: _____

Accessories color: _____

Favorite items: _____

Special nook: _____

Place to entertain: _____

Lighting: _____

Storage: _____

Sensory appeal: _____

KITCHEN

Paint color: _____

Accessories color: _____

Favorite items: _____

Special nook: _____

Place to entertain: _____

Lighting: _____

Storage: _____

Sensory appeal: _____

FAMILY ROOM

Paint color: _____

Accessories color: _____

Favorite items: _____

Special nook: _____

Place to entertain: _____

Lighting: _____

Storage: _____

Sensory appeal: _____

....

DINING ROOM

....

Paint color: _____

Accessories color: _____

Favorite items: _____

Special nook: _____

Place to entertain: _____

Lighting: _____

Storage: _____

Sensory appeal: _____

....

OFFICE SPACE

....

Paint color: _____

Accessories color: _____

Favorite items: _____

Special nook: _____

Place to entertain: _____

Lighting: _____

Storage: _____

Sensory appeal: _____

OUTDOOR SPACE

Paint color: _____

Accessories color: _____

Favorite items: _____

Special nook: _____

Place to entertain: _____

Lighting: _____

Storage: _____

Sensory appeal: _____

GUEST BEDROOM

Paint color: _____

Accessories color: _____

Favorite items: _____

Special nook: _____

Place to entertain: _____

Lighting: _____

Storage: _____

Sensory appeal: _____

FORMAL LIVING ROOM

Paint color: _____

Accessories color: _____

Favorite items: _____

Special nook: _____

Place to entertain: _____

Lighting: _____

Storage: _____

Sensory appeal: _____

BASEMENT

Paint color: _____

Accessories color: _____

Favorite items: _____

Special nook: _____

Place to entertain: _____

Lighting: _____

Storage: _____

Sensory appeal: _____

GARAGE

Paint color: _____

Accessories color: _____

Favorite items: _____

Lighting: _____

Storage: _____

Sensory appeal: _____

ELSIE'S FAMOUS BLUEBERRY MUFFINS

Makes 1 dozen

1½ cups flour	¼ cup (½ stick) butter, softened
½ cup sugar	½ cup milk
2 teaspoons baking powder	1 egg
½ teaspoon salt	2 cups blueberries (frozen)

FOR TOPPING

⅓ cup sugar	2 tablespoons butter, melted
¼ teaspoon cinnamon	

Preheat the oven to 400 degrees F. Line a muffin pan with cupcake liners or grease with butter.

Mix the dry ingredients in a small bowl. In a medium bowl, beat the butter, milk, and egg. Beat in the dry ingredient mixture. Gently stir in the frozen blueberries. Scoop the batter into the muffin cups. Bake for 25 minutes or until the tops of the muffins begin to brown. Remove from the oven and cool for 10 minutes.

To prepare the topping, mix the sugar and cinnamon in a small bowl. Put the butter in a second small bowl. Dip the top of each muffin in the melted butter, then in the cinnamon-sugar mixture.

Elsie Juhasz, Dan's grandmother, was a beloved baker of Old World pastries in Cleveland, Ohio. Elsie's blueberry muffins, a family tradition, add a special touch to any brunch . . . or housing negotiation. We hope you love them as much as we do.

INDEX

ABOUT THE AUTHOR

ALI WENZKE and her husband moved ten times in eleven years, living in six states across the U.S. Now she helps the millions of people who move each year by providing practical tips on how to build a happier life before, during, and after the move on her blog, *The Art of Happy Moving*. Ali is happily settled in the Chicago suburbs with her husband and three children. She doesn't plan on moving anytime soon. *The Art of Happy Moving* is her first book.